Movement

From Person to Actor to Character

Theresa Mitchell

The Scarecrow Press, Inc.
Lanham, Md., & London
1998

SCARECROW PRESS, INC.

Published in the United States of America
by Scarecrow Press, Inc.
4720 Boston Way
Lanham, Maryland 20706

British Library Cataloguing in Publication Information Available

Library of Congress Cataloging-in-Publication Data

Mitchell, Theresa, 1955–
     Movement : from person to actor to character / Theresa Mitchell.
          p.   cm.
     Includes bibliographical references and index.
     ISBN 0-8108-3328-X (alk. paper)
     1. Movement (Acting)   I. Title.
PN2071.M6M55   1998
792′.028—dc21   97-14861
                                                      CIP

♾ ™ The paper used in this publication meets the minimum requirements of
American National Standard for Information Sciences—Permanence of
Paper for Printed Library Materials, ANSI Z39.48–1984.
Manufactured in the United States of America.

Contents

Preface — v

Acknowledgments — vii

Introduction — 1

PART ONE: BODY AND CARE — **3**

Your Body: Structure and Function — 5
   The Skeletal System / The Head / The Spine / The Rib Cage / The Shoulder Girdle / The Arm / The Pelvis / The Thigh / The Knee / The Lower Leg / The Foot / The Muscles / Muscle Strength / Muscle Coordination / Muscle Soreness / Summary / Journal Entries

Actor as Athlete — 19
   Warming Up / Cooling Down / Warm-up: Person to Actor to Character / Athletic Training: Endurance, Strength, Flexibility, and Diet / Endurance / Strength / Flexibility / Diet / Injury Prevention / Summary / Journal Entries

PART TWO: PERSON TO ACTOR — **25**

Relaxation — 27
   Relaxation: Person to Actor / Relaxation: Person / Relaxation: Actor / Summary / Journal Entries

Alignment — 31
   Alignment: Person / Alignment: Actor / Placement / Lengthening and Widening / Summary / Journal Entries

Breath — 39
   Breath: Person / Breath: Actor / Images / Phrasing Breath with Movement / Summary / Journal Entries

Center — 47
   Center: Person / Center: Actor / Summary / Journal Entries

Sound and Movement — 51
   Sound and Movement: Person / Sound and Movement: Actor / Summary / Journal Entries

Imagery — 55
   Color / Seasons / Essence / Elements of Nature / Animals / Music / Nonmusical Sounds / Events / Summary / Journal Entries

Space, Time, Weight, and Action — 63
   Qualitative Space / Quantitative Space / Direction / Levels / Range of Motion / Spatial Relationships / Qualitative Time / Quantitative Time / Qualitative Weight / Quantitative Weight / Action / Dynamics and Intensity / Summary / Journal Entries

Environment, Properties, and Costumes   73
Environment: Person / Environment: Actor / Properties / Costumes / Shoes / Garments / Summary / Journal Entries

PART THREE: CHARACTER   **79**

Character and Relaxation   81

Character and Alignment   83

Character and Breath   85

Character and Center   87

Character: Sound and Movement   89

Character and Imagery   91

Character: Space, Time, Weight, and Action   95
Space and Character / Time and Character / Weight and Character / Action and Character / Summary / Journal Entries

Character: Environment, Properties, and Costumes   99
Environment / Properties / Costumes / Summary / Journal Entries

Case Studies   103
Relaxation and Character   103
Alignment and Character   104
Breath and Character   105
Center and Character   105
Imagery and Character   106
Space, Time, Weight, Action, and Character   106
Environment, Properties, Costumes, and Character   107

Conclusion   109

Bibliography   111

Plays Cited   113

Index   115

About the Author   119

PREFACE

The concept of movement as an individual discipline has evolved and become diversified in the actor training programs of many universities and conservatories. Directors, acting teachers, and movement specialists have tried to identify what movement for the actor means, and what movement training should include. The current responses to these questions are as diverse as the discipline itself. Some believe that the path to developing an expressive and communicative body lies in the study of techniques such as mime, dance, circus skills, stage combat, martial arts, and yoga. Others form a foundation for movement training on F. M. Alexander's or Moshe Feldenkrais's methodologies. All of these disciplines offer the actor valuable skills, heightened self-awareness, and more informed body usage.

There are a variety of available texts addressing these techniques that are helpful and resourceful for movement studies. This text utilizes resources from some of these disciplines and offers another means of connecting movement to acting. The primary thrust is to go beyond physical development and skill by processing movement from person to actor to character.

This text presents a guide for the actor and teacher in developing characterizations that are connected to thought, word, and action. The actor who goes beyond physicality and technical proficiency will be responsive to impulses connected to emotions, needs, ideas, and desires, which will bring life to a character.

Exercises and projects for better understanding physical and psychological connections in relationship to movement choices are the focus of this text. Part One introduces the body's structure and health maintenance. Part Two presents basic elements of movement, application through exercises, and the connection between the person and actor in character preparation. Part Three implements exercises and creative projects with character stud-

ies. The case studies chapter is designed to provide focus for analyzing a variety of characters from well-known plays and to be used as references for the projects in Part Three. The plays range from ancient Greek to contemporary American. While the beginning acting student might not be ready to work on a classical scene, the characters and plays cited provide rich lessons and may be used as models for contemporary studies or for advanced acting challenges in the future.

This text is of value to actors, directors, and teachers who wish to use movement as an impulse for characterization. It is designed for actors and teachers who focus on movement, characterization, and scene study. It is written in the voice of a teacher addressing an acting student. Ideally, the text is used for one year in a classroom environment, but can also be used independently. Sections of the text may be lifted for a shorter term of study, or can be expanded upon for more than a year's course work. It is recommended that the movement concepts be explored in the order presented because one principle builds upon another. It has been utilized in this manner in both small and large liberal arts theatre arts programs, as well as in a first-year conservatory class. However, individualistic approaches to the study of acting and movement may alter the process sequence.

I first explored many of the exercises in workshops, classes, and during rehearsals. I owe a great portion of the material to former teachers and directors, for whom I have the utmost respect and admiration. The knowledge I gained through their teachings allowed me to discover and enhance my own ideas. It is my hope that the ideas presented here will provide stepping stones for new impulses in the movement-for-actors arena.

ACKNOWLEDGMENTS

Over the years many students, teachers, friends, and family members have shared their wisdom and offered support. Their reflections as well as my own are in this book. I wish to especially thank Mary Sparks for her constant encouragement, questions, answers, attention to detail, and laughter. I thank Lucinda Holshue for her creative spirit and sharing it with me. The following teachers and friends have significantly influenced the ideas and exercises presented in this book: Jennifer Martin, Marcia Douglas, Kenneth Washington, David Barker, Denise Myers, Joan Schirle, and Tom Casciero. Thank you to my students, friends, and colleagues at the Conservatory of Theatre Arts at Webster University for continually challenging my perceptions of theatre and life. Thank you to Mark Mitchell who has always been a part of my spirit.

INTRODUCTION

Imagine that you have just been cast as Laura in Tennessee Williams's *The Glass Menagerie.* You are familiar with the script and understand the character's inability to cope with the harshness of reality. You have studied her relationships with the other characters and are ready to begin rehearsals. It is at this point that your real task begins. How do you, as a vibrant young actor, capture Laura's fragile essence and create outer physical manifestations that will communicate her inner reality? Movement principles are complex, and there are a number of methods you can choose to undertake. Whatever method you utilize, it is important to first make some discoveries about personal movement patterns.

The acting process is comprised of an interlocking trinity: the person, the actor, and the character. As a person, you have habits and idiosyncrasies that are unique and have been cultivated over the years in response to your life experiences. As an actor you may have developed another set of behaviors that manifest themselves when you are actually performing. The actor is an extension of the person. While acting you may have a heightened awareness of your physical and expressive behaviors. At the center of each character is the contribution of the actor and the fulfillment of the person.

The character you choose to create is comprised of basic human elements—experiences, desires, and emotions—and, as such, is considered every bit as complex as a "real" person. It is an actor's challenge to identify the character's needs, and discover similarities and differences from self. These needs can be pinpointed within the script or through discussion with a teacher or director. Ultimately, it will be your objective to discover the origin of the character's needs, experiences, and emotions, and channel them into movement and behavior.

Part One of this text addresses the complexities of the human structure and its maintenance. Part Two is directed to the search and acknowledgment of the many facets of your personal and artistic self,

so that appropriate qualities may be channeled into characterization, which is addressed in Part Three. The case studies chapter outlines a variety of characterization projects from a wide range of plays. This is for your reference as you move through the projects in Part Three. You might choose to use the character studies with specific projects outlined or choose others more suited to your needs.

The building of a character may seem a daunting task; however, by utilizing the resources already present within yourself you will find the needed tools. The bridging process from person to actor to character is a key component of character development. While you cannot totally "lose" yourself within the character you are portraying, you can learn to identify personal traits you have as an individual and as an actor that are congruent with the character's make-up and use them to your advantage. By the same token, you may discard those personal habits that do not serve you as an actor and for a specific characterization. The exercises within this text will guide you toward making the necessary choices needed to achieve the extension of self to character. How does one go about completing this task? That is the focus of this text. As you explore each section, you will find exercises designed to help you solidify the movement concepts presented. While reading books about acting will not make you an actor, physically practicing what you discover in your reading may generate new ideas and develop into working skills.

Space is provided at the end of each chapter to record your thoughts. Keeping a journal solidifies thoughts, perceptions, and questions, and provides a record for continued growth. It is a place to process connections between movement and acting. The journal space is a place to record your observations, discoveries, questions, and answers for future reference. It can provide a rich record to return to after several years of study as it becomes a treasure of your knowledge.

Acting is about making choices: physical, emotional, and intellectual. As you work through the exercises, you may find that you need to be making choices about simple things that you previously took for granted. Initially, some exercises may feel awkward because they invoke an awakening of a previously dormant area. Being uneasy with a new way of moving is to be expected. Expect the unexpected. The more you work through the exercises, the more spontaneous you will be, and the more focused your work will become.

The choices you make as an actor cannot be designated as right or wrong. They merely indicate where you are in the midst of your discovery process. Learning a variety of concepts and techniques serves to widen your field of choices, thus enhancing your creative abilities. A word of caution: Don't seek immediate gratification or results from the exercises. Not every exercise will work for every actor; try to approach each one with an open mind. These exercises are designed to explore the discovery process rather than guarantee a finished product. After you have gained an understanding of the concepts illustrated adopt those that work for you. Use the journal sections to record and process which exercises will be beneficial for your future needs.

Acting, like life, is in a constantly dynamic state. The events that occur each day in your life cause changes within you, and with each change comes growth. Growth increases your acting choices and process. With the help of this text, perhaps a teacher, and a strong sense of dedication on your part, you will learn to use these changes in making stronger and more developed acting choices through movement.

Part One

Body and Care

A subtle movement can be as expressive as poetry. To learn how to create a movement as meaningful as a sonnet, you need to learn the language of the body. Primary study of the body as a communication tool begins by addressing basic human anatomy, physiology, and health maintenance issues.

Part One outlines the human structure and its function, and how to take care of yourself. The actor's two communication tools are the body and voice. Learning about your potential resources and communication skills will provide a foundation for discovery. You will have a basic understanding of your body's mechanics and health needs. The knowledge you acquire will be used for the rest of your life. It will not only contribute to your acting process, but will also help you to take care of your body so you might have a longer life and career.

YOUR BODY: STRUCTURE AND FUNCTION

Begin your movement studies with an overview of your physical resources. The human body is an amazing network of bones, muscles, and connective tissues. Knowledge about basic physiology and anatomy will help you understand your body's structure and function. You will be more perceptive about a movement's origin, initiation, and motivation. Your observations of behavior, nonverbal communication skills, and physical analysis will be heightened.

Knowledge of the physical self is helpful in maintaining a healthy lifestyle through good nutritional habits and exercise. Injury prevention and understanding how to care for your body when it is stressed can be essential for an extended acting career. It is important for all people to be healthy, but for an actor it is crucial. If the body is weak or unable to function properly the actor is at a loss to perform at maximum potential.

THE SKELETAL SYSTEM

To begin, look at the body's framework and what holds it together. The framework is the skeletal system, which is formed by more than two hundred bones. The connection between two bones is a joint. A hinge joint enables two bones to flex toward each other. The elbow and knee are hinge joints. A ball joint enables a wider range of rotation. The hip and shoulder are ball joints. Each joint has a specific function and is designed for particular movements. When a joint is misused it becomes stressed and may lead to injury. The possibility of avoiding injury is increased with knowledge about the design and function of your body. The bones and joints are supported, stabilized and moved by muscles, tendons, and ligaments.

As an actor it is not necessary to be able to iden-tify each bone, but it is beneficial to have an understanding of the arrangement and function of the skeletal frame. The skeleton is like a finely engineered building. Each unit supports another unit, and whenever one segment is misused or out of alignment, the whole structure suffers. Each section of the body will be examined individually, while keeping in mind the structure as a whole. Use the illustrations as a reference.

THE HEAD

Examine the features of the head. It weighs from twelve to fifteen pounds, and its proportionally small base (the top of the spine) calls for a fine sense of balance. Examine where the base of the skull connects to the first vertebra; this is the occipital point. The skull and spine are joined by connective tissues: muscles, tendons, and ligaments, which provide support and mobility. The spinal structure and flexible connective tissues provide complex movement capabilities.

Follow these suggestions while examining the movement potential for each body part.

1. Start with slow and evenly controlled movements.
2. Locate the movement's origin.
3. Acknowledge your physical and psychological responses to the movement.

Responses to movement may vary each time a movement is performed. It is valuable to acknowledge psychological, sensorial, intellectual, and emotional responses to physical changes as they occur. This helps you connect the physical and psychological experiences and expressive behaviors in preparation for character studies.

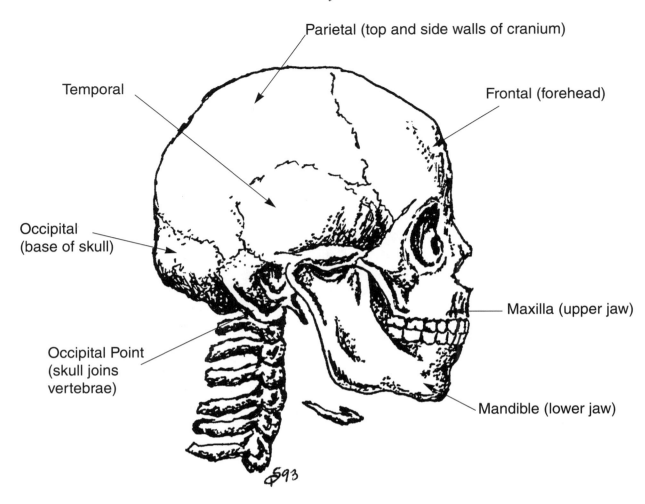

Parietal (top and side walls of cranium)

Temporal

Frontal (forehead)

Occipital
(base of skull)

Occipital Point
(skull joins
vertebrae)

Maxilla (upper jaw)

Mandible (lower jaw)

SKULL AND CERVICAL VERTEBRAE

Exercise: Head Isolations

A. Forward and Back

1. Tilt the head forward and back. Extend from the crown of the head and/or the occipital point so the cervical spine is not collapsed. Gently release the head forward until the chin is near the chest.
2. Lift the head upright.
3. Let the head gently release back. Concentrate on lifting out and away. Avoid grating the vertebrae against each other.
4. Continue releasing the head forward, lifting to center and releasing back.
5. As you move through each motion sense the physical and psychological response.

B. Side to Side

1. Tilt the head to the side. Release the head toward the top of the shoulder and look straight ahead.

2. Lift to center.
3. Tilt to the other side. Focus on elongating the spine.
4. Continue exploring the movement slowly from side to side. Breathe with the movement and sense how the movement informs perception.

C. Head Rolls

1. Tilt your head to one side.
2. Release the head to the front and to the other side so the head completes a semicircular pattern.
3. Bring the head up to center.
4. Repeat the semicircular pattern, but start on the opposite side.
5. Gently release your head to swing side to side.
6. When your neck muscles have released tension, move your head through a circular pattern. Keep elongating the spine by using an upward directional energy flow from the tailbone through the crown of the head.

Exercise: Gestural Head Expressions

1. Stand facing a partner at approximately an arm's distance. Focus on each other's head and neck.
2. One at a time, move the head slowly in any direction. Stop the movement and sustain the position. If you are in motion, note the physical and psychological connection. If you are the observer, note your interpretation of the movement. Share your insights.
3. Continue until you have explored a variety of positions and motions.

Exercise: Movement Potential of the Head

1. Randomly move the head in several directions. Start slowly and smoothly before moving with various tempos and types of movements, like bouncy, lyrical, jerky, and swinging. To prevent injury, warm-up the neck muscles before making any repetitive or sudden movements. Keep the direction of the head moving away from your center to minimize spinal pressure.
2. Initiate physical activity from the head. Walk, sit, jump, run, skip, read a newspaper, etc. Start slowly so you can sense the movement impulse and be aware of the follow-through. As you move, describe the sensations associated with movement.

THE SPINE

The head is supported by the spinal column, which is composed of twenty-four small bones called vertebrae. The spine can be divided into three sections: the cervical vertebrae are the top seven and the most flexible; the thoracic vertebrae are the middle twelve and connect to the rib cage; and the lumbar vertebrae are the bottom five, which allow forward and backward movement. The sacrum is below the last vertebrae and is wedged between the hip bones.

You can feel the spine's back ridge with your hand. Each vertebra is separated by a cushion of cartilage that prevents friction and absorbs shock. Use the following exercises to heighten awareness of your spine and movement potential.

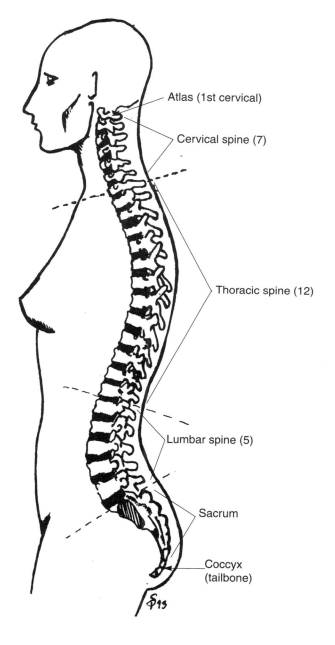

Atlas (1st cervical)

Cervical spine (7)

Thoracic spine (12)

Lumbar spine (5)

Sacrum

Coccyx (tailbone)

SPINE

Exercise: Spinal Articulations

1. Pair up with a partner, and select who will be partner A and B.
2. Partner A stands in a relaxed position. B stands behind A, places the outside hand on A's shoulder, and uses the other hand to massage the spine. This will provide stabilized contact. Keep the contact firm and even.
3. Partner A slowly rolls down from the top of the head to completely hang over at the hips. B massages the soft tissue surrounding each vertebra as A releases forward. After A is completely relaxed over, B massages A's lower back for a further release of tension.
4. Partner A slowly rolls up as B reverses the process by massaging from the lumbar base to the spine's top vertebrae. Move slowly to fully experience the movement with heightened awareness.

Exercise: Spinal Articulations

Exercise: Rag Doll

1. Stand in a balanced position.
2. Relax your head forward and bend the knees.
3. Roll down vertebra by vertebra until the crown of your head is pointed toward the floor. Relax all the way over from the hip joints, not the waist.
4. Gently pulse from the knees and release tension.
5. Slowly roll up to standing, stacking one vertebra on top of the other until you are upright and looking straight ahead.

Exercise: Movement Potential of the Spine

1. Stand in a comfortable position with the legs and arms uncrossed.
2. Slowly alter the spine's shape to create different alignments. Maintain each position long enough to register a physical and psychological response.

Exercise: Spinal Articulations

Exercise: Spinal Articulations

What are your responses? How does a physical shape provide impulses for a psychological state? How can these discoveries be channeled into actor and character choices? Write in your journal and process your impressions.

THE RIB CAGE

The rib cage is joined to the twelve thoracic vertebrae and provides a protective covering for your heart and lungs. Because of the flexible connection with the spine and support of the intercostal muscles, the rib cage has mobility to expand, rise, and lower during movement. The rib cage's movement potential includes side-to-side, forward-and-back, and circular motion capabilities.

Exercise: Rib Isolations

1. Using a wide stance, place your hands on your hips.
2. Isolate the rib cage and shift it to one side. Bring the rib cage back to center and shift to the other side. Repeat several times.

3. Start from center and isolate the ribs, moving them forward, center, and back. This motion is often more difficult than from side-to-side and may need to be performed with greater awareness.
4. Isolate the rib cage and move it in a circular pattern, shifting to front, side, and back. Move slowly and try to isolate the rib cage and spine.

When attempting to isolate one section of the body, tension may shift into another body part. Continue to scan the entire body for unneeded tension. If you begin to hold tension try releasing it with deep breaths or by gently shaking it out. The exercises in the relaxation section may provide relief for common tension problems.

Exercise: Movement Potential of the Rib Cage

1. Start in a balanced stance and move the ribs slowly in random directions. Arrive at a new body position based on rib cage placement.
2. Sustain a position, and in a semi-audible voice describe your sensations. Are the sensations physical, mental, or emotional? How do these physical behaviors inform mental and emotional responses?
3. Discover how many different shapes you can create by shifting your rib cage. How does each stimulate a new sensation?

THE SHOULDER GIRDLE

Shoulder tension is very common and can be lessened through awareness, observations, and knowledge about structure and function. The clavicle (collarbone) and scapulae (shoulder blades) are bones included in the shoulder girdle. The clavicle consists of two narrow bones extending from the sternum (breastbone) connecting the neck to the upper arms. This area can be lifted and dropped independently of the shoulder blades, which are not attached to the body by any joint but are held flat against the back of the rib cage by muscles lying over and under them. The shoulder girdle provides the bony framework to which the arms are attached.

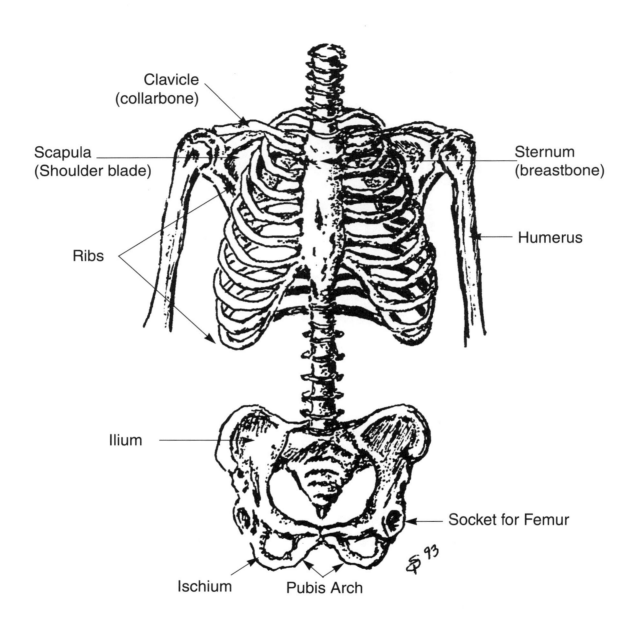

Clavicle
(collarbone)

Scapula
(Shoulder blade)

Sternum
(breastbone)

Humerus

Ribs

Ilium

Socket for Femur

Ischium   Pubis Arch

TORSO AND PELVIC GIRDLE

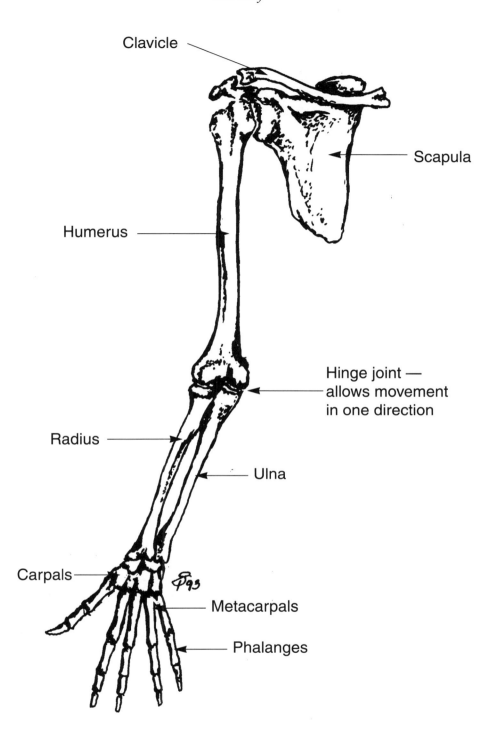

Clavicle

Scapula

Humerus

Hinge joint —
allows movement
in one direction

Radius

Ulna

Carpals

Metacarpals

Phalanges

SHOULDER AND ARM

Exercise: Shoulder Isolations

1. Lift the shoulders straight up toward the ears.
2. Release the shoulders back to center and then press the shoulders down.
3. Move the shoulders in a large circular motion.
4. Press the shoulders forward to separate the shoulder blades as much as possible. Hunch forward.
5. Press the shoulder blades together toward the spine. Arch back.
6. Roll one shoulder at a time and then simultaneously in various directions.
7. Stop the motion in different positions. Note any responses you have regarding the body's shape and attitudes created.

THE ARM

The humerus is the largest bone in the upper body. At the top of the humerus is a ball joint that connects the arm to the shoulder blade. This ball joint allows the upper arm extensive range of motion. The humerus joins with the bones of the lower arm, the radius and ulna, at the elbow. The elbow hinge joint enables the lower arm to bend toward the upper arm.

The hand is connected to the forearm at the wrist by several types of joints, which enables the hand to move in many directions. The hand's structure makes it one of the most complex functional body parts. Each finger has three joints, and the thumb has two. This enables the hand to make numerous gestures.

Exercise: Movement Potential of the Arm

1. Move an arm in various directions.
2. Isolate the wrist's movements.
3. Explore many different finger movements.
4. Move the entire arm in random motions. Pause in various positions and note any responses. The responses may be psychological, emotional, intellectual, or sensorial.

THE PELVIS

The sacrum, or tailbone, is connected to the bottom of the spine. Two large hipbones flare out from the sacrum and turn in at the center to form a cup-like shape, with a large opening at the bottom. This total structure is the pelvis. On each side of the hipbone, below the ilium, is the ball-and-socket joint that links the pelvis to the thighbone. The multiple connections between the spine, hip, and thigh bones allow the pelvis a wide flexible range.

Exercise: Pelvic Isolations

1. Stand with your feet at a comfortable distance apart and bend the knees. Align the knees over the toes.
2. Slowly shift your hips front to back, side to side, and in a circular motion. Isolate the pelvic movement from the upper torso.
3. Move the pelvis through random positions, and note any responses associated with physical changes. Process your responses in your journal and/or through discussion.

THE THIGH

The femur, or thighbone, is the longest and strongest bone in the body. Its head is in a ball shape that fits into a socket within the pelvis. The ball shape provides front-to-back mobility for walking, side-to-side motion, and limited rotation.

Exercise: Movement Potential of the Thigh

1. Lie on your back and lift your right knee toward your chest. Let go of unnecessary tension. Concentrate on isolating the femur's movement in the hip socket. Move the thigh in various directions.
2. Bring both knees toward the chest, and move the thighs in circular motions. Allow the joints to move freely. Be aware of where the movement begins.
3. From a standing position, gently swing a leg forward and back. Experience the movement in parallel (feet, knees, and hips on a front-to-back plane), and in a turned-out (femur rotated away from the center) position. Swing the leg from side to side, in a turned-out position.
4. Heighten your awareness of the thigh's movement potential as you walk, sit, march, skip, run, jump, or execute other locomotor activities.

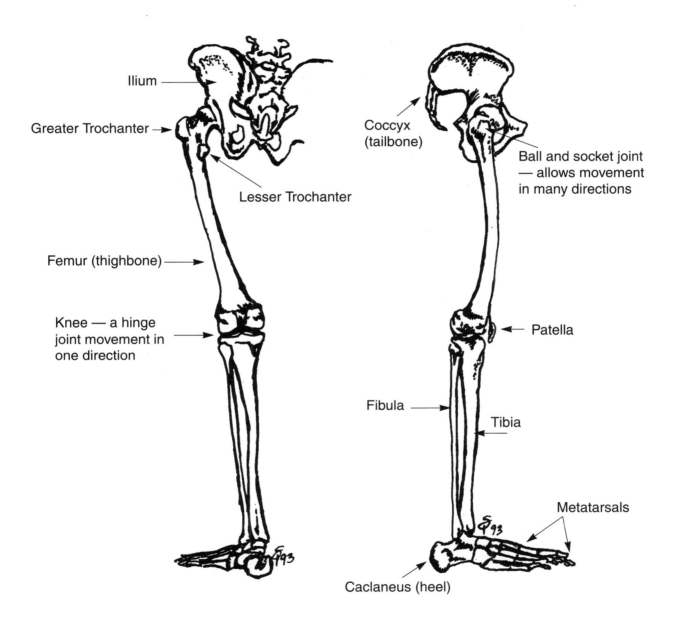

Ilium

Greater Trochanter

Lesser Trochanter

Femur (thighbone)

Knee — a hinge joint movement in one direction

Coccyx (tailbone)

Ball and socket joint — allows movement in many directions

Patella

Fibula

Tibia

Metatarsals

Caclaneus (heel)

PELVIS AND LEG: back and side view

THE KNEE

The knee is a delicate joint and needs proper alignment to prevent injury. It is a hinge joint, which allows movement in only one direction. Knee injuries often result when the knee is pressed in an unnatural lateral motion. At the front of the knee is the patella or kneecap, which is a small loose bone. This is attached to the lower leg by ligaments (fibers that connect bone to bone) and a tendon (a band of tough tissue connecting muscle to bone).

Exercise: Alignment of the Knee

1. Stand in a balanced position with the feet in parallel. Feel an equal distribution of weight on the toes, balls, and heels.
2. Perform small knee bends. Make sure the knees are aligned directly above the feet to prevent injury.

Caution: If the knees roll in toward or away from each other, there is a risk of injury to the ligaments and tendons. The body is a work of architecture, and improper stress on the foundation may result in life-long problems. A major point of these explorations and discoveries about the physical structure and function is to heighten your awareness of how the body is designed for healthy movement. Learn to listen to your body. It will signal when it feels stress or strain.

THE LOWER LEG

Two parallel bones connect the knee to the ankle: the tibia (shinbone) and the fibula (calfbone). Though they are equal in length, the tibia alone connects the joint at the knee. The fibula is attached to the under surface of the tibia's wide head. At the lower end both bones hang free to form the ankle joint.

Exercise: Movement Potential of the Ankle

1. Sit on the floor with your legs extended.
2. Flex your feet by pulling the toes toward you.
3. Point your feet by stretching the toes away and to the floor.
4. Raise the leg slightly off the floor and rotate the ankle and foot. Discover the multiple articulations possible.

THE FOOT

The foot is strong enough to support the entire body because of its unique structure. It has twenty-six bones set in a semicircle, forming an arch. The arch absorbs much of the impact of your body's daily stresses, such as walking or jumping. The foot's motion is aided by flexible toes (metatarsal), which also provide balance.

Exercise: Movement Potential of the Foot

1. Sit with your legs extended in front and isolate your toes' movements by flexing, pointing, and clutching.
2. Stand and arch one foot, leaving only the toes and ball of the foot on the floor. Lift the thigh and press the toes off the floor so the foot is pointed. Return the foot to the floor by rolling the toes, then the ball of the foot, and finally the heel onto the floor. Repeating this action will help strengthen the entire foot. Reminder: Align the shoulders, knees, and feet.
3. Walk slowly and notice the action and response. Use your journal to record impressions.

Awareness, understanding, and knowledge of your physical structure and function will take time and effort. Over time a mental concept of the physical self takes shape. This self-image may be inaccurate owing to low self-awareness and to life-long misuse of the physical structure and function, and therefore is not easily corrected in a short time-span. Having a teacher guide you through the understanding of the body is invaluable, but if you choose to do these explorations on your own, be patient and willing to repeat the exercises as many times as necessary to form a more accurate body image. If you discover poor body usage take time and effort to slowly develop healthier movement patterns.

THE MUSCLES

The skeletal system is connected and covered by muscles, tendons, and ligaments. The skeleton provides the body's framework, and the muscles perform the actions.

There are more than six hundred individual mus-

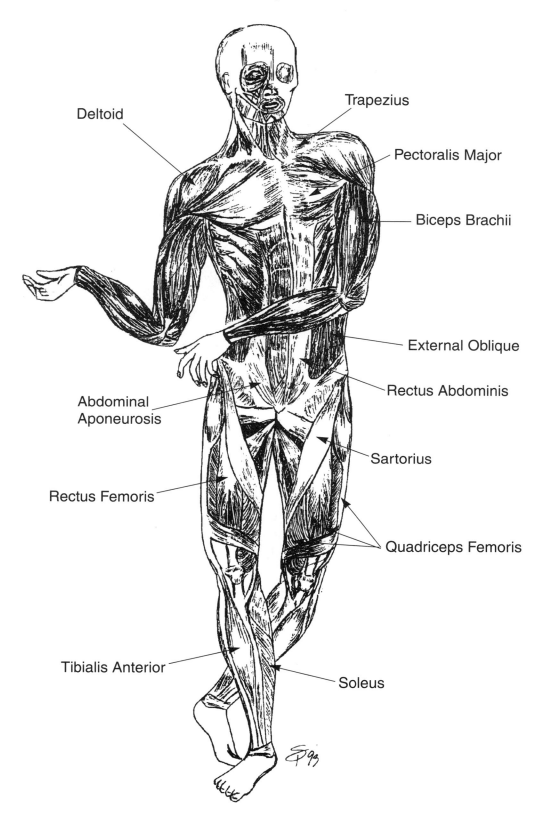

Deltoid

Trapezius

Pectoralis Major

Biceps Brachii

External Oblique

Rectus Abdominis

Abdominal
Aponeurosis

Sartorius

Rectus Femoris

Quadriceps Femoris

Tibialis Anterior

Soleus

MUSCLES OF THE BODY: front view

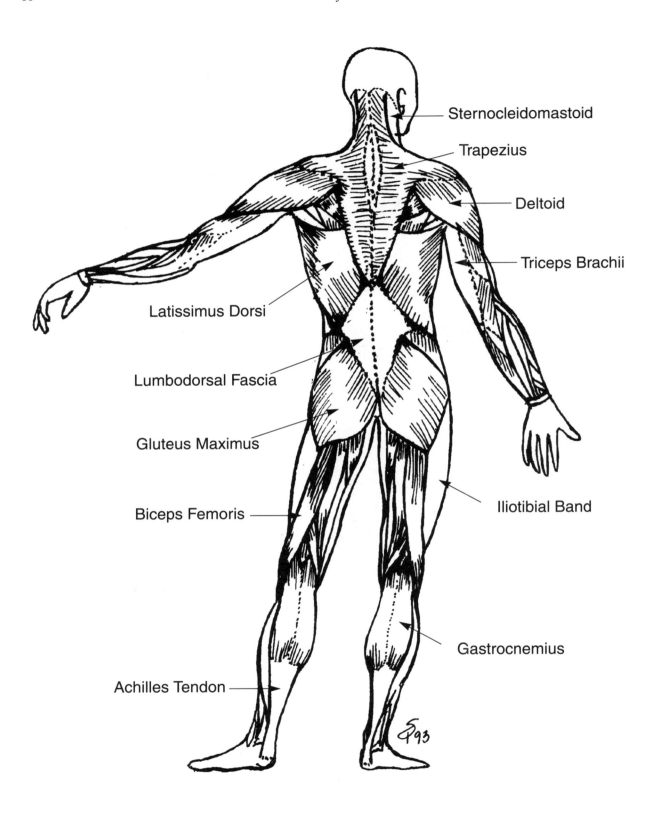

Sternocleidomastoid

Trapezius

Deltoid

Triceps Brachii

Latissimus Dorsi

Lumbodorsal Fascia

Gluteus Maximus

Biceps Femoris

Iliotibial Band

Gastrocnemius

Achilles Tendon

MUSCLES OF THE BODY: back view

cles that support and move your body. Muscles are composed of stringy fibers bound together in bunches. The bulk of the muscle is fleshy and can contract and expand like a piece of elastic. Tendons connect muscle to bone. Ligaments connect bone to bone. The muscles, tendons, and ligaments comprise the body's connective tissue.

Muscles move in pairs. An initiating muscle is called a prime mover, and the responding muscle an antagonist. When the biceps are the prime movers and contract in an effort to bend the arm, the triceps respond as the antagonist and release. When the triceps contract, the biceps release and the arm straightens. If one muscle group is not balanced in relationship with the opposing group, tension may increase. It is important to establish a fitness program that activates many muscles, and not isolate a few, for conditioning over an extended time period. Vary your exercise program for greater strength, flexibility, and range of motion.

Muscles change their shape when flexing and contracting. A muscle never completely relaxes, and though you may be motionless, your muscles are always active. This is muscle tone, and it keeps your body in a continual state of readiness. Many of the exercises in following chapters call for releasing unneeded tension. This means being prepared for movement, with minimal tension.

MUSCLE STRENGTH

A muscle can be strengthened by repeatedly using it at maximum force during a series of repetitions. Strength training activities should push the muscles to fatigue in order to be valuable. The point of fatigue is reached when the exercise cannot be repeated safely or properly. This is not to be confused with the "no pain, no gain" theory, which can result in preventable injury. If pain is experienced, stop exercising and evaluate your physical usage. It may be that you are misusing the physical design.

Challenge yourself with progressive degrees of difficulty, each requiring greater force or resistance to increase your strength. You might not need or have the time for an intensive strength conditioning program. However, even minimal strength conditioning is beneficial and can improve stamina. Further discussion about strength training is included in the chapter "Actor as Athlete."

MUSCLE COORDINATION

Muscle coordination depends upon a highly complex nervous system. Given a healthy start in life you learn to coordinate your movements until you master basic locomotor skills such as walking and running. To increase your proficiency and coordination train the muscles through habitual practice of challenging skills. At first you may feel clumsy when learning a new movement, but with regular practice the muscles will become more efficient and responsive. This enables you to learn dance patterns, stage combat sequences, play sports, or engage in any other activity that requires coordination. It is best to learn new movement patterns slowly to avoid frustration.

MUSCLE SORENESS

It is almost inevitable that your muscles will become tender and sore when you exercise vigorously. If the muscle is sore because of weight training or another activity that stresses the muscle tissue, you will need to rest the muscle for up to thirty-six hours and repeat the conditioning process. Muscle soreness usually decreases in a few days. There are several approaches you can take to facilitate healing. These remedies include, but are not limited to: massage, applied moist heat, gentle stretching, and warm baths. For more serious pain, you should consult your physician. Listen to your body.

SUMMARY

The skeletal system and connective tissues are much more complex than this chapter outlines. The terminology and descriptions are simple and meant to provide a working knowledge of your structure and function that can be used immediately. By better understanding the body's structure you will begin to discover movement potential rather than limitations. You will have a better understanding of how to care for your body so that you might avoid injury and stress and improve your physical condition. Give yourself time to sharpen your physical awareness and you will be better prepared for acting challenges.

JOURNAL ENTRIES

What are your impressions about linking physical movement to psychological responses? What responses are primary for you (physical, emotional, intellectual, psychological, sensorial, etc.)?

Describe any new discoveries or observations about your physical awareness or condition. What would you like to maintain or change?

What part or parts of your body are you most or least comfortable moving and why?

Process additional observations, impressions, and ideas for future reference.

ACTOR AS ATHLETE

Like an athlete, an actor must push the body to its highest potential regularly to accomplish the best performance possible with a sense of artistry and satisfaction. The body must be cared for through discipline in the preparation and performance phases of activity. The preparation phase consists of proper physical training. This includes warming up, pushing the body to its limits through a planned physical conditioning program, following through with a cool-down, maintaining a healthy diet, responding to recuperative needs, and self-awareness for injury prevention. The more you know about your body the better prepared you will be to physically train and prevent injury. A key factor for injury prevention is warming up.

WARMING UP

An actor can learn from well-trained athletes the benefits of reviewing basic physical activities required to heighten performance. Athletes often begin conditioning with a warm-up to prepare for strenuous activity. The warm-up may be generalized or specific. A generalized warm-up consists of a series of exercises that prepare the body for a wide range of activities. It might be a set routine that includes raising the body's core temperature, loosening the joints, stretching and strengthening the muscles, and increasing the heart rate, which pumps more oxygen into the body tissues.

If you regularly use a set routine, be conscious of the movements to receive the maximum benefit from your efforts. It is also vital to maintain physical awareness to prevent injury. You will gain the most from the warm-up by performing the activity correctly and by incorporating a full range of motion.

A specific warm-up is designed for a particular activity or character that has special physical demands. It might include preparation for a dance or fight sequence, or a period style. While working through this text you will discover individual physical traits for characterizations. These unique traits, combined with possible special physical skills for a given character and production requirements, may increase the benefits for a specific warm-up.

A warm-up not only prepares the body for action, but also the mind. It focuses and centers the self for a rehearsal or performance. It is important to connect the mental to the physical, including the voice, during the warm-up. If your warm-up is habitual self-awareness must be heightened so you avoid moving through the warm-up on automatic pilot and underuse your movement potential. Use images to connect spontaneous physical responses, and utilize your self-awareness. This is much the same as knowing your lines of dialogue and required physical activity for a production and being responsive to new stimuli for each performance.

A warm-up should:

1. Prepare the mind and body for a rehearsal or performance.
2. Raise the body's temperature by increasing blood flow to the muscles and heart.
3. Loosen the joints and increase the range of motion.
4. Stretch the major muscle groups.
5. Contract major muscle groups to increase control and strength.
6. Assist in achieving a sense of being that is centered and ready to respond.

As you study acting, voice, movement, or any physical training program, you will be introduced to a myriad of exercises you may want to use in a warm-up. Your generalized warm-up will change as your body changes. Use the six goals above as a guide to create a warm-up that works for you.

COOLING DOWN

Cooling down is a transition from an activity and/or character portrayed back to your daily self. The transition should be gradual, paralleling your decrease in heart rate to a normal resting condition. It should be done immediately following a workout, rehearsal, or performance as you return to a restful state. It is an important time to acknowledge and honor your work. By doing so you respect your art and self, and can be objective about your growth as an actor and athlete.

The cool-down should be structured according to the activity completed. If you performed a physically demanding role you need to bring yourself back to a balanced state that will minimize the stress on the body and prevent injury. Likewise, if it was a mentally taxing performance take time to refocus or center yourself. You will feel better about your acting and self.

Anytime you engage in conditioning it is important to keep a positive attitude. Thoughts are energy. When the energy is positive it is easier to focus and make steady improvement. A positive attitude will make new possibilities of movement more accessible, as well as heighten mental and physical self-perception.

WARM-UP: PERSON TO ACTOR TO CHARACTER

A warm-up can help you make the transition to meet performance requirements. Listen to your body, mind, and spirit. Locate areas of unneeded tension and release. What activity will help you prepare, focus, and center? Find your range of motion and increase it through the warm-up. Focus both mentally and physically. You are your own best teacher in terms of actual perception about yourself. You are aware of your physical condition, and have the resources to make needed adjustments. Acknowledge what you feel at the beginning of a class, rehearsal, or before a performance, and set a goal for what you would like to feel by the end. Design a warm-up that suits your personal needs and record it in your journal.

After you warmup on the personal level, decide if you need a specific warm-up for a performance or rehearsal. As an actor, do you have any particular physical, vocal, or psychological needs that might be served through a warm-up? What exercises would prepare you? A basic understanding of your needs as an actor will be explored in exercises in Part Two, and will assist you in choosing those that will help you prepare for performance.

Each character has specific behaviors. Structure part of your warm-up to prepare for the character. Acknowledge your personal experience and the desired adjustments for a characterization. How can you prepare the body to adopt the character's physical qualities in a healthy way? What can you do to harmonize the body, mind, and spirit during a warm-up? How you can bring yourself to the character in an efficient and healthy manner?

ATHLETIC TRAINING: ENDURANCE, STRENGTH, FLEXIBILITY, AND DIET

The subjects of endurance, strength, flexibility, and diet are interconnected. If you focus on endurance, strength, or flexibility you will likely improve the other two areas at the same time. A healthy diet will advance the conditioning process.

Endurance

Endurance training involves improving your circulatory and respiratory systems. It will increase your energy resources while preparing you for stressful productions and physically demanding roles. Improving the oxygen flow through the body is like fueling a fire with air. The more air the fire receives, the hotter the intensity of the flames. You can learn to adjust the amount of energy needed for a vital performance depending on the characterization and physical activity required. The key is to have the resources within yourself to create the most exciting performance possible. If you have the desire but not the energy, the creative process will be frustrating.

Endurance training increases the strength and size of the heart's muscles. To do this, elevate your heart rate to 60–80 percent of its maximum capacity per minute for twenty minutes a minimum of three times per week. The maximum heart rate is calculated by subtracting your age from 220. Then, calculate 60 percent and 80 percent of your maximum heart rate to find your training target range. For example, if you are twenty, then your maximum heart rate is two hundred beats per minute. Multiply two hundred by .60 and .80 to find the target heart rate range of

120–160 beats per minute. After ten minutes of exercise, calculate your heart rate by taking your pulse for ten seconds and multiplying it by six. Check your heart rate every ten minutes. Modify movement to stay within the target range. Be sure to cool down after elevating your heart rate for an extended period of time. Use this chart for simplified calculations:

Age	Target Heart Rate
20	120–160
25	117–152
30	114–140
35	111–142

If you prefer not to use the standard target heart rate, you can be aware of your breath during a workout and aim for a vigorous breathing cycle while still being able to talk. If you cannot speak because you are nearly out of breath, then you are training too hard and need to slow down or modify your workout.

There are many activities you can participate in to improve your endurance. Consider dance training or a martial art as techniques directly connected to skills demanded for the stage. Both improve self-awareness, alignment, concentration, sense of form, and coordination skills. Other activities that will improve your endurance are walking, swimming, bicycling, and most competitive sports.

Rotate training methods to avoid burnout or boredom. It is more beneficial to condition with an activity you enjoy rather than one you force yourself to go through. It is also better to rotate training techniques to condition various muscle groups rather than to overtrain the same muscles.

Other benefits of endurance conditioning are:

1. Stress reduction
2. Lowered resting heart rate
3. Improved use of nutrients
4. Weight control

Endurance training relieves stress because as oxygen is pumped to the muscles they heat up and relax. If you add stretches to your workout you will be able to increase flexibility and become more kinesthetically alert. Your resting heart rate is lowered because the heart muscle is strengthened, requiring fewer beats to pump blood through the heart chambers. As the muscle becomes stronger it takes less effort for it to contract, thereby reducing the resting heart rate. You will be able to perform longer and be less fa-

tigued. Endurance training also helps the body use food more efficiently. It assists the bones in maintaining healthy calcium levels. Activity builds muscle tissue, which uses more fuel than fat tissue. The more you exercise the better the body will utilize nutrients.

STRENGTH

Improving muscle tone and strength to meet the demands of performance is beneficial in actor training. The muscles should be conditioned to be responsive and capable of meeting the requirements of daily and professional activity with minimal stress. Lifting small free weights, such as dumb-bells, for many repetitions may be best suited for an actor because endurance is achieved as strength improves. Use equal resistance while lifting and releasing. Complete up to three sets of twelve to fifteen repetitions. The muscles may be fatigued, which signals that they have been stressed to the maximum and need rest to rebuild. Rest for thirty-six hours so the tissue can recover and strengthen. Increase the weight moderately as your strength improves. A high number of repetitions will support endurance training because the heart rate will rise with the activity. If you do not have access to free weights or weight machines, perform isometric exercises.

Strength exercises focus on muscle contraction. This can be troublesome for the actor who is habitually tense. Use stretching exercises in conjunction with strength conditioning to lessen tension and muscle contractions. If you stretch and strengthen the muscles you will build muscle tissue that is both strong and supple and be able to perform a wider range of activities. If you work only on strength you will develop tight muscles that might restrict movement. If you only stretch the muscles may be weak and vulnerable to injury.

FLEXIBILITY

Each person's flexibility depends on their age, health, and body structure. During the early years you are more limber because the muscles have not been stressed to the degree that is experienced later in life. As you mature your joints take longer to release tension and your muscles tighten as the complexity of your daily activities mounts. Your health plays a major role in your flexibility. The healthier your diet, level of exercise, and conditioning, the more resilient your body will be.

Flexibility can be measured by range of motion in joints and muscles. Every joint has its own range of motion. One hip or shoulder joint may be more flexible than the other. You can increase your flexibility through regular exercise, so it is important to exercise daily to gain maximum movement potential.

Raise the body's core temperature before you stretch. As the body tissues warm up they will be more pliable and the joints will release. To prevent injury it is important to breathe fully during strenuous exercise and have a heightened awareness of the entire body.

There are two major types of stretches: ballistic and static. Ballistic stretches, sometimes referred to as "bounces," contract and release the tissues in a repetitive manner that should be avoided. Static stretches sustain the stretch at a maximum degree. Hold a static stretch for ten seconds to give the muscle and connective tissue time to release the contraction with minimum stress. Static stretches will produce less muscle soreness and be less stressful. Ballistic stretches are likely to cause injury and have little conditioning value.

It is better to stretch larger muscle areas like the back, thighs, and upper arms before stretching small areas such as the neck, calves, and forearms. Larger muscles need less subtle movements than the smaller and more delicate muscles and joints. This type of training also means changing from a generalized focus to a more concentrated one.

There are also two methods of stretching: passive and active. Passive stretching is when you are stretched by a person or machine. This enables you to focus on alignment, form, and breath. Passive stretching is good to use when building a relationship with another actor. It opens lines of communication and increases sensitivity through shared activity. Active stretching is when you actively engage muscles without the assistance of a person or machine. You use your own strength to complete the full range of motion and release into the stretch. A key to active stretching is to reach your maximum potential through self-discipline. Stay in tune with what you are experiencing and record your growth.

The benefits to a regular stretching program are:

1. Improved freedom of movement
2. Increased range of motion
3. Improved circulation
4. Less muscle tension
5. Stimulated muscles and minimized fatigue
6. Improved joint mobility

If you combine a flexibility training program with strengthening and endurance you will feel better about yourself. You will have a greater physical motion range. Most of all, you will improve the connection between your mind, spirit, and body.

DIET

The word diet elicits images of denial, aggravation, and misery. Instead, it should mean healthy and sensible nourishment that provides the energy resources needed to maintain a hectic and possibly unpredictable schedule. It will benefit you to understand how the body is structured and how to maintain your physical and mental self through sound nutritional practices. You know that your body requires fuel to function. The question is, what types of fuel will provide the most effective nutrients? An essential factor for good nutrition is variety and balance. Eat a variety of foods every day. Maintain a food journal by recording everything you eat and drink for a week, then analyze the nutritional balance. The food guide pyramid found on many food products (especially cereal and bread products) may be used as a reference for the analysis. This exercise can reveal nutritional patterns over a given time period.

Water is an essential part of a healthy diet. The body is primarily water. In Jane Brody's *New York Times Guide to Personal Health,* she calls water "the most essential nutrient" and points out, "Your blood is 83 percent water; your muscles 75 percent; your brain 74 percent; your bones 25 percent; and your body fat 20–35 percent." With so much of the body composed of water, the importance of maintaining an adequate supply is evident. Most nutritionists recommend drinking an average of sixty-four ounces of water each day.

There are hundreds of books on nutrition available at bookstores and libraries. Read about good nutritional habits and make them part of your daily activity. Avoid fad diets or unbalanced eating habits. These will only leave you fatigued and frustrated. A balanced diet will better prepare you for rehearsal and performance demands.

INJURY PREVENTION

The first step in preventing injuries is to carry through all physical activity with an alignment, placement, focus, breath, and sense of self-awareness each of which is appropriate for the movement. Injuries often occur because of physical misuse. That is why it is important to have an understanding of your body and its potential and limitations. The second major cause of injury while training or performing is overuse of some part or all of the body.

Injuries might be prevented if you heighten your physical awareness. When an action feels tense or painful—stop. Review the motion sequence and how it was executed. Are you pushing your body to do something it is not prepared or equipped to accomplish? Are you misusing the body through poor alignment or placement? Be sensitive to your body's needs and defenses. If you are in a production and unable to complete a movement as directed because of a physical condition, speak to the director immediately and make arrangements for the action to be completed in another manner. If it is a problem related to lack of knowledge about how to execute the movement correctly, ask for a movement coach or some assistance so you can avoid injury. You are responsible for your health care and maintenance.

To prevent injury approach a new physical activity at a slow pace. Learn the movement sequence and analyze how it might be carried through with minimal stress. Be patient. Practice a complex movement several times at a moderate tempo before executing it at full speed. By doing so the body is trained to execute the movement correctly, and you are less likely to misuse the body when the adrenalin of performance is added.

SUMMARY

The comparison of actors to athletes is longstanding. It is valuable for actors to learn from the discipline of great athletes. Most return to basic training techniques regularly to sharpen their skills. They practice daily, and do not take their bodies and talents for granted. Like an athlete the actor must care for the body. Learn to listen and respond to its needs. Condition the body through daily exercise and maintain a healthy diet.

If you have a limited background in exercise and nutrition, read and take classes about the subjects. Numerous resources about diet and health are available. Use common sense when selecting a program and materials by looking for ones that encompass long-range plans and goals.

Project a future image of yourself. Where do you want to be, what will you be doing, and what will be the condition of your body, mind, and spirit? Plan how you will accomplish your goals. Be disciplined, and be patient.

JOURNAL ENTRIES

Design a generalized warm-up. Make it approximately twenty minutes long. Use exercises or games from past experiences that work for you, or create a movement sequence based on your physical perceptions and needs. Use the guideposts listed in the warm-up section of this chapter.

Describe several ways to cool down after a strenuous activity or a performance.

Describe your approach to endurance training. What is your goal?

Assess your strength. If you were to make any improvements in this area what goals would you set?

What areas of your body are flexible? In which areas would you like to improve flexibility?

Record your diet for one week. Include all beverages. Review the diet while using the food pyramid as a basis of good nutrition. How can you improve your eating habits and health?

List any injuries that you need to be aware of when moving. What can you do to protect yourself from re-injury?

Record additional observations, impressions, and ideas for future reference.

Part Two

Person to Actor

The center of an acting experience is drawn from personal interpretation. Your personal interpretation is shaped by years of habitual behavior with idiosyncratic characteristics. To expand movement potential and acting choices, you need a clear definition of self. The actor is an extension of the person. Acting heightens physical, mental, and spiritual awareness. Senses are sharpened. You become more centered, focused, and vulnerable when acting. The ability to draw from your personality and imagination are enhanced as you make character choices. Part Two offers exercises designed to enhance personal movement potential and acting choices in preparation for characterization.

As you move through the exercises, keep an open mind and a sense of discovery. There is not a correct or incorrect outcome or expectation for any exercise. Nurture a sense of play. Be childlike. Your growth will be unique and need not be compared with others for this process. Each person has special traits and qualities that are honored and acknowledged. Build on your personal strengths so a solid foundation is created for your acting process.

RELAXATION

It may seem strange to begin the technical practice of a movement process with the study of relaxation, since movement is associated with energy and motion, and relaxation with passiveness. However, relaxation for the actor does not mean a total release of the muscles, but rather implies a state of readiness in which unnecessary tension has been minimized and the actor is prepared to act. Although a certain degree of tension is required for movement, it is the unneeded or excess tension that blocks creativity and physical responsiveness. It may take years to become fully aware of the ways you misuse your body. What may feel "right" and "natural" has been conditioned through years of habitual usage. A teacher or guide can provide an objective viewpoint to assist your awareness. However, much can be gained through self-guidance and practice. Take a few minutes each day to relax and release. You will develop healthier patterns and usage over a short time period.

RELAXATION: PERSON TO ACTOR

Relaxation enables channels of thought, emotion, and physical sensitivity to open. Many people do not allow themselves to fully realize their intellectual, emotional, and physical capabilities because they have blocked those resources with tension. By identifying tension, you can begin to reduce stress to free your imagination. Creative energy that can be channeled into dynamic character choices is more accessible during relaxed states. Relaxation is movement without unnecessary stress that blocks mental and physical creativity. You can transform unnecessary tension into creative energy, which will lead to dynamic movement. This creative energy will help you better understand yourself before creating and adopting a character's behaviors.

Begin with relaxation methods to locate areas of personal tension, both mental and physical. Assess your tension habits as an actor. The tension caused by daily stresses may be different than the stresses that surface when acting. Once you have located areas of unnecessary tension in your personal life and as an actor, you can begin to concentrate on the appropriate relaxation/tension, energy, and dynamics for a character.

Begin with relaxation exercises designed to assist in locating tension that prevents you from achieving maximum movement potential in your personal life. Several exercises outlined here have proved effective. Numerous relaxation methods are available. Search out new ideas, investigate, and practice. Decide what is the best approach for you to reach an energized and relaxed state.

Start with exercises for which you lie on the floor. The floor supports the body, relieving the muscles from stress. You can concentrate more fully on the physical self when few demands are being made on it. Distinguish between unnecessarily tense muscles, energized muscles, and passively relaxed muscles.

RELAXATION: PERSON

Exercise: Relaxation Through Breath

1. Lie on your back with your knees bent and your feet flat on the floor at a comfortable distance from your buttocks. Rest your back on the floor. Place your arms close to your sides with the palms up.
2. Focus on your breath flowing in and out. Let it flow in through the nose and out through the mouth with your lips slightly parted. This is a cleansing breath. Let your weight drop into the floor. Imagine that the floor is a cradle, a safe place to rest.
3. Stay alert and notice how little effort is

required to rest in this position as you drop your weight into the floor. Focus on taking the first step toward tension awareness and release. Your objective is to become energized and relaxed.

Exercise: Relaxation Through Scanning

1. Scan the body for tension. Begin with the head and work through one area at a time until you reach the toes. As you inhale visualize the breath flowing into an area, scooping up the tension, and exhaling the tension with the breath. Repeat a cleansing breath for each area and release tension.
2. After you have used breath to cleanse yourself of unnecessary tension repeat the process, but this time let the breath energize each area. You may want to try various images, for example, imagine the breath tickling the muscles, massaging them, or recharging their energy cells with gentle electrical currents.

Exercise: Progressive Relaxation

This exercise is a stress management staple. Perform progressive relaxation twice a day for a week. By doing so, you will sensitize yourself to unneeded tension. The more you practice progressive relaxation, you will begin to know when you are excessively tense doing daily activities, rehearsing, and performing. For example, you may become aware of jaw tension during a rehearsal and be able to release the tension with a breath and simple message, and continue your activity.

1. Settle into a comfortable position. Loosen your clothing. Stretch and yawn. Give your weight to gravity.
2. Inhale and tighten every muscle in the body and hold for five seconds. As you release the muscles release the breath and say, "Release and let go." Acknowledge the sense of relief and slip into a deeper relaxed state.
3. Wrinkle your forehead, tighten the jaw, and make your face very small by contracting all the facial muscles. Hold the tension for five seconds, keeping the rest of the body limp. When you exhale, release the tension and say, "Release and let go."

4. Repeat the sustained tension on the inhale and release on the exhale for each body area.
5. After progressing through the entire body focus on releasing and repeat, "Release and let go." Become more and more relaxed with each exhale.
6. Return to cleansing breaths and heighten your kinesthetic awareness so that you might learn to recognize a relaxed state more readily.

Exercise: Autogenic Relaxation

Johannes Schultz, M.D., and Wolfgang Luthe, M.D., developed the autogenic relaxation technique, which is a means of self-regulating stress. Practicing this technique will quickly enable you to release tension with a thought or image.

1. Lie in a comfortable position.
2. Focus on your breath rolling in and out like ocean waves. Repeat several times, "My breath is calm and refreshing." Feel waves of relaxation roll through the body.
3. Repeat to yourself: "My body is heavy and warm." Allow the message to become true.
4. Shift your focus to your right hand and arm. Repeat several times: "My hand and arm are heavy and warm." Next, turn your attention to the left hand and arm and repeat the message.
5. Move your attention to the right leg and foot. Imagine your breath moving into the leg as you repeat: "Warmth is flowing into my leg and foot. They are becoming heavy and warm." Repeat with the left leg and foot.
6. Allow your focus to include both arms and legs. Repeat several times: "My limbs are heavy and warm. I am becoming more and more relaxed with each breath."
7. Focus on your torso as you breathe in and say, "I am calm. My chest is open and relaxed."
8. Imagine channeling breath through the entire body and repeat: "I am calm and peaceful."
9. Count to three and become more alert with each number. Open your eyes, stretch, and yawn on "three."

After practicing autogenic relaxation you will feel calm and refreshed. Perform relaxation exercises slowly so that you can become sensitive to changes. If you rush the process you may miss important movement qualities that can help you later.

Exercise: Schmurzing

"Schmurzing" is a nonsense term used to describe the physical sensation this exercise creates.

Lie down and begin to stretch in all directions. Breathe deeply and yawn. Stretch for a few minutes, shake out, and let your body settle into the floor with the knees bent and the feet resting on the floor.

This exercise loosens the joints and muscles. In the previous exercises, the joints have been largely inactive. To loosen a joint, gently move it in slow motion. Rotate the joint until it is supple. See if you can move from schmurzing to an energized and relaxed state while using cleansing breaths.

The Rag Doll exercise described in the chapter "Your Body: Structure and Function" may be used for relaxation, alignment, and centering. The better your alignment and sense of being centered is, the easier it will be for you to shed unnecessary tension. The next working phase of relaxation is to relax while standing.

Perform the Rag Doll exercise daily until you reach a kinesthetic sense of a balanced stance that requires minimal tension. After you begin to feel actively relaxed while standing, scan the body for unnecessary tension. Release tension with breath or by stretching and shaking.

Once you are aware of the minimal tension needed for standing, begin to focus on walking, sitting, and gesturing. Take time to review your movements for each activity, and sense whether stress and tension can be reduced while maintaining energy.

Exercise: Imaging

From your earliest moments of consciousness, your imagination has been active. Unfortunately, it may have been dulled by societal pressures and demands as you matured. The following exercise is designed to stimulate the imaginative impulse in the interest of relaxation.

1. In a comfortable position, either sitting or standing, visualize a warm, pleasant image. Let the image flow into all parts of your body. Stay in contact with the present as you allow yourself to become one with the image. Possible images could include a warm tropical beach; immersing yourself in a pool of warm liquid; or wrapping yourself in a comforter before a glowing fire on a winter night. Create detailed images so they become "real." Let yourself experience a relaxation response.

2. Experience the world the image has created, and visualize yourself being active within the image. Visualize yourself wanting something and pursuing your desires.

The exercise will release muscle tension while your mind is creating images. Your body, mind, and spirit will be stimulated simultaneously.

Work with various images to see how they affect tension levels—cool, soft, peaceful, colorful, etc. Stay with pleasant images. Let your breath and body respond to each image. The exercise is not solely for the purpose of energized relaxation but to acknowledge the needed tension level depending on the idea and/or action. By identifying appropriate tension levels in response to a particular activity, you can begin to bridge personal tension identification and appropriate character tension and dynamics. Before you do this, examine the types of tension created when acting.

RELAXATION: ACTOR

You may experience a degree of tension that occurs specifically when you are in front of an audience. Much of this tension is the result of stage fright. It may manifest itself in various forms, such as a tight knot in your stomach, a constricted throat, tightened shoulders, trembling hands, or weak knees. Stage fright symptoms are numerous, but the important idea is for you to identify your own list of tension habits that occur repeatedly when you perform.

Keep a journal of your performance experiences. Are there repeated instances of inhibiting tension that are created regardless of the character you are portraying or the performance situation? These are anxieties that you can learn to identify and alleviate through exercises. Suppose your jaw becomes tense whenever you perform. It is obvious that this could prevent you from performing to your best ability. Practice exercises designed to make you conscious of the difference between a released and tensed jaw and how you can release the jaw when you feel it is unnecessarily tensed.

Exercise: Telling a Story

1. Tell a story to one person.
2. Acknowledge and note any tension you experience as you tell the story. If tension surfaces, ask when, where, and how it began. How did it manifest itself?
3. Tell the story to a larger audience, and notice whether the tension changes, and how. Ask the others what they observed.

This exercise can help you acknowledge the tension you feel when you are acting. As you become aware of tension and the problems it can create you can begin to find solutions by knowing what relaxation techniques work for you—autogenic, progressive, use of images, breath, stretching, or any relaxation technique of your own design.

Relaxation is a basic premise for a solid acting technique. It has long been utilized as a key to unlocking creativity. Leaders in various disciplines related to the acting process have long been aware of the positive attributes of a relaxed state of being. In *Freeing the Natural Voice,* Kristin Linklater cautions, "Vibrations are murdered by tension." While Linklater is addressing the use of the voice, the same principle applies to movement. Movement begins with energy and vibrations. When the body is strained by tension it will not realize its full movement potential.

Exercise: The Seven States of Being

This exercise is adapted from the teachings of Jacques Lecoq. It examines the differences between three levels of tension. Explore each state and connect physicality to psychology. Let breath and sound flow from the movement. Be able to identify the varying degrees of intensity from one state to another.

A.	Level One: Relaxed	Below Relaxation
		Leisure
		Economical
B.	Level Two: Dramatic	Dramatic Action
C.	Level Three: Contraction	Pipe Cleaner
		Aluminum
		Iron

Below Relaxation is the lowest level in the relaxed state. In this state of being, the muscles have very little structural tension. The body moves as if it were a rag doll or a marionette. While bobbing around in space, the body remains limp. Imagine that the bones are soft and flexible, that the muscles are heavy and warm, and that when you move it is without strain.

The **Leisure** State suggests a level of tension that is "laid back." There is more structural tension than in Below Relaxation, but the body moves very loosely. The bones are slightly more rigid and the muscles more dense.

The **Economical** state is very efficient. No movement is performed for the sake of moving or without reason. Each move is purposeful. The bones are firm and the muscles relaxed yet actively responsive.

Dramatic Action is the state of being when everything is important and dramatic. You are alert to everything happening around you. You are ready for anything. You are like a cat, ready to pounce in any direction in a fraction of a second. You are sensitive to stimuli. You are ready to make choices. You feel a need to communicate. You are ready to perform. This state of being is the bridging of person to actor. The joints and muscles are fully active.

Pipe Cleaner is a state of tension in which the body becomes stiff, yet is very movable and can be shaped. Unfortunately, many actors find themselves in this state when they are tense. The joints are slightly restricted and the muscles tight.

Aluminum is a state of greater tension than Pipe Cleaner. Joint movement is halted, the speech pattern is affected because the jaw is less mobile, and the muscles are very tight.

Iron is the last state of tension. This level of tension allows for minimal movement. The body freezes and it is difficult to react spontaneously. Muscles and joints are rigid.

Explore each state of being for physical and psychological responses. Start with the Below Relaxation state. Lie down and let your muscles release. Imagine that you have very soft bones and your muscles are like gelatin. Lift an arm and let it go; it is dead weight. Lift a leg or your head. There is minimal tension when you move. Roll over. Sit up. Move various parts of your body. Give yourself motivation to stand. What are you experiencing? Be as specific as possible. Give yourself motivation to walk, sit, and do everyday activities. Your jaw is released and your eyes are soft. Your focus may be fuzzy or indirect. Explore the space. Let sound release from the physical expression. Interact with someone. Do not mime anything, just indulge in the state of being and respond to stimuli. Go to your own space and play with the text of a nursery rhyme or a short poem. Let the movement influence the voice and interpretation. Let go of expectations and be in the moment.

What did you discover about movement and expression in this state of being? What were your physical and psychological connections? What happened to the interpretation of the nursery rhyme or poem? Record your responses in your journal.

Move through the other states of being in a similar manner. Begin in a restful position. Let the state of being infiltrate your body, mind, and spirit. Explore the state of being with various parts of the body, then move through space. Engage in daily activities and with others. Add the use of texts. Process the experience and record your impressions in the journal.

Make clear distinctions between each state of being. Move around and sequence the seven states together, then alternate between the states in random order. Connect sound with movement. You are fully expressive in each state.

After completing these segments of the exercise, go back and concentrate on the differences among Economical, Dramatic Action, and Pipe Cleaner states. These are the three most common degrees of tension. More often than not, you want to find Dramatic Action and be able to return to it each time you perform. However, the state of being may be altered depending on the needs of a specific character. This exercise and others will be applied to character studies in Part Three.

SUMMARY

In order for you to explore choices about a character's physical dynamics first acknowledge personal tension areas, both as an individual and an actor. Once you have located unnecessary tensions and have avenues for attaining a healthy state of relaxation, you can begin to apply the concept of tension dynamics to character development in later studies. Use your observation skills and heighten your awareness and availability of choices. It is best to have a teacher and guide to provide insights about your levels of tension and how they are manifested. Trust your teacher's

perception. Often someone else will be able to visually pinpoint unconscious habitual tension.

JOURNAL ENTRIES

In what body areas do you experience habitual and excess tension?

What relaxation techniques work for you and why?

Describe any performance anxieties that are troublesome. What relaxation technique would better prepare you for rehearsals and performances?

Describe your physical and psychological responses during the seven states of being explorations. How did the interpretation of your nursery rhyme or poem change from one state to another?

Record and process your observations, impressions, additional relaxation techniques, and ideas for future reference.

ALIGNMENT

Alignment refers to the arrangement of the skeletal and muscular systems in an efficient and balanced order. If the skeleton is aligned properly it will require very little muscular effort to support the body in a standing position. When one part of the skeleton is misaligned, unnecessary muscular tension is created and the entire body is affected. The body needs to function as a whole unit and not as individual parts.

In Part One the skeletal and muscular systems were reviewed. The relationship of one body part to another was examined, along with how the head rests on the top of the spine, how the pelvis connects to the base of the spine, how the legs connect to the hips and support the pelvis, and how the entire frame rests on the feet. With this in mind, when you look at a skeleton you will notice how perfectly the human architecture is designed. It is when the body is pushed into unnatural forms of alignment that unnecessary stress is created and the ability to perform is hindered.

Alignment is often associated with posture. Posture suggests a fixed body position. One example is the "straight back": The shoulders are pulled back, causing the chest to push forward, the abdomen is pulled in with the buttocks tucked under, and the knees are locked. This is sometimes known as a "military stance." Besides being hazardous to your health, this is not what is meant by alignment. A healthy alignment is not something that can be captured in an ideal stance and copied. Each person's alignment is as different as each person's body. It is not something that can be achieved and held in a fixed position, but must be in motion and alive. A healthy alignment is the sequential arrangement of the bones supported by the muscles in a harmonious union.

What may feel harmonious, natural, and right may be an alignment that has slowly developed over many years and is, in fact, a misalignment. Because you have habitually moved in the same manner over time, the movement feels natural. When you begin the process of eliminating poor habits, it feels unnatural and wrong. You should be aware that old habits that took time to create will also take time to modify. It is ideal to have a teacher guide you with hands and eyes for many of these exercises. An objective person who can guide you through the process will help you understand the differences between natural and habitual physical use and misuse.

ALIGNMENT: PERSON

Before you can adjust your personal alignment to create a character's heighten your personal alignment awareness. This will make you more perceptive about your physical patterns formed through habitual usage. It is difficult to be objective about yourself, and even more difficult to be impartial about activities and feelings that have been so reinforced through daily practice that they are no longer conscious manifestations. If you have a teacher to guide you through these exercises, use their hands and vision for the needed objectivity. If your are working alone, move slowly and tune into a total body awareness. Be observant when muscles tighten and joints lock. Breathe and release.

Exercise: Acknowledging Your Alignment

1. Stand facing a full-length mirror. Do not try to alter any part of your body; just observe. Look at the position of the feet, knees, hips, ribs, shoulders, arms, hands, neck, and head. Shift to other stances. After each, acknowledge the physical and psychological sensations.
2. In profile, stand with what feels like a healthy alignment. Turn your head and look at yourself in the mirror. Acknowledge your alignment from your feet to head. Look for hyperextended knees, a tilted pelvis, a collapsed or

expanded chest, shoulders that slump or arch back, and a chin that juts forward or pulls back. Look for broken angles on the vertical axis.

3. Pair up with a partner and observe each other from the front, side, and back. Review your observations with your partner. Model your observation.

Exercise: Walking Alignment

1. Pair up with a partner.
2. Walk away and back toward your partner several times. The partner should make a detailed observation of the walk and be prepared to imitate it.
3. Become aware of the manner of your walk. Discover where the weight is placed. What is the movement of the arms, hips, and head? Where is your focus? What is your energy like? How and where do your heels hit the ground? Do not try to alter the walking pattern, but acknowledge the movement.
4. After you have walked away and toward your partner several times, your partner begins to closely follow you and identifies with the movement characteristics and manner through imitation. When you feel the essence of your walk has been captured, stop, and begin to observe. What aspects of yourself does your partner model?

This exercise can enlighten by providing an outside frame of reference for your alignment and adding to your awareness of how you project your physicality.

Exercise: Alignment During an Activity

1. Prepare a three-to-five-minute activity that involves standing, walking, and sitting. Do the activity without dialogue. Be yourself.
2. Perform the activity for observers.
3. Observers, share thoughts about the alignment used in the activity. Be objective, and without using commentary or judgment describe in simple terms your observations. Listen to the observations to learn more about your image and alignment without attempting to justify or defend. If a video camera is available tape the stance from the front, profile, and in motion.

Replay the tape to examine alignment patterns.

ALIGNMENT: ACTOR

Once you acknowledge your personal alignment, you can build a neutral alignment as a foundation for character study. A neutral alignment is one without obvious structural characteristics suggesting personality. Neutrality offers the advantage of a solid foundation when building a character. In *Building a Character,* Constantin Stanislavski used the analogy of "starting with a clean canvas when painting a picture." By doing so you start with fewer layers of personal habits. Many exercises throughout this text start with a neutral stance. It is a safe place to take off from and return to when exploring new behaviors. A neutral stance requires minimal effort so it opens mental and physical pathways otherwise blocked by unnecessary tension. Neutral is when space, time, and weight efforts are resting, but are ready to ignite and intensify.

Moshe Feldenkrais and F.M. Alexander are proponents of neutral states. In *The Actor Moves* Claudia N. Sullivan states: "Feldenkrais' method allows for development of 'zero position.' Zero position also denotes an absence of personal movement cliches, idiosyncratic ways of standing or tension in a particular part of the body. This position is an advantageous, relaxed but energetic starting point for the actor." In her article "The Alexander Technique as a Basic Approach to Theatrical Training," found in *Movement for the Actor* Aileen Crow writes: "When performers can come to a 'divine neutral'—a state in which the self is well balanced, flexible, and adaptable—they can become clear channels for the ideas they wish to express."

Exercise: Neutral Stance

While there are many directives in this exercise, avoid unnecessary tension. Let your energy flow rather than attempt to hold a "correct" position or stance.

1. Stand with your hands relaxed at your sides. Place your feet approximately four to six inches apart with the toes pointing in the direction of the knees. Align your heels with your shoulder blades if you need a point of reference.
2. Relax your feet into the floor. Let the balls of the feet, toes, and heels support equal weight.

It is best to work barefooted or in soft-soled shoes without a heel.

3. Bend your knees slightly and align them directly above the toes. Straighten the knees, but do not lock them by pushing them back and clenching the muscles around them.

4. Check for any unnecessary tension in your feet, ankles, knees, and pelvis. Use deep cleansing breaths as you scan for tension.

5. Let your tailbone drop toward the floor. Do not try to tilt the pelvis forward or back, but concentrate on the tailbone being gently released downward.

6. As the tailbone is dropped, lengthen your spine upward. Think of a shaft of light pouring up and out from the base of your spine through the top of your head. Let the light seep in between each vertebra. Energy is flowing up and down the spine.

7. Let the opposition of the tailbone dropping toward the floor and the crown of the head floating up toward the sky lengthen your spine. The feeling should be one of motion, and not a static position. Keep breathing deeply and be ready to move.

8. Let your shoulders drop down. Release the shoulder blades downward as you continue to lengthen your spine.

9. Scan for any unnecessary tension in your abdomen, buttocks, back, chest, and shoulders. Continue deep breath cycles.

10. Let your arms hang from your shoulders. There should be very little tension in your arms, elbows, wrists, or hands. If you notice any tension, give the arms a gentle shake and let them drop into place. Your spine is lengthening from top to bottom.

11. Check for unnecessary tension in your jaw. Let it drop open. Do not force it open. Let your facial muscles release.

12. Scan for any unnecessary tension from your head to your toes. Continue deep cleansing breaths. Let breath flow into an area, pick up tension, and release on the exhale.

Go slowly and concentrate. Through repetition, you will be kinesthetically sensitive to the neutral feeling and be able to return to it quickly.

The Rag Doll exercise helps you become sensitive to the feeling of neutrality and a healthy alignment. Rolling down through the spine and releasing the tension, and then rolling up, stacking one vertebra above another and letting parts of your body drop into place is the best way to attain a healthy alignment and a sense of neutrality. Perform the Rag Doll exercise three times, and after each time use the checklist given in the Neutral Stance exercise to scan for problem areas. The body should feel light, open, balanced, and ready for activity.

PLACEMENT

Placement of weight is determined by the vertical position of the body in space. The weight of the entire body should be shifted slightly forward. There will be a little more pressure on the balls of the feet than on the heels. The entire foot remains in contact with the floor. The knees remain relaxed along with the rest of the body. With the placement forward, the actor is better prepared to move in any direction, and the body tends to lift and stay open rather than crunching downward.

Exercise: Placement

1. Perform the Rag Doll exercise three times and finish in a neutral stance.

2. Shift your weight slightly forward from the ankles. Make your body one unit in the weight shift. In other words, shift the entire frame, not just the hips, chest, or head.

3. With your weight forward, slowly walk around the space. Return to a neutral stance.

4. Shift your weight back on your heels and walk. Return to neutral. How does walking differ when the placement is forward as opposed to back?

5. Shift your weight in various directions, and each time move about the space. Try walking in several directions, stopping and going, and sitting. Compare all of these placements and how they affect your movement and its initiation.

LENGTHENING AND WIDENING

Too often, the stresses of daily problems build tension in the back, causing it to pull down and contract. This is also a protective reaction against danger. This contraction becomes habitual. You need to observe and avoid this type of alignment. Instead, feel your spine and torso lengthen and widen with energy. The sensation may feel like you are taller. The following exercises are designed to heighten kinesthetic awareness as the spine releases.

Exercise: Body Extension

A cautionary note: When working with a partner and physical adjustments, stay attentive to your partner's experience. Do not move quickly, jerk, or startle your partner. Keep the actions smooth and subtle. Communicate with each other.

1. Pair up with a partner.
2. Partner A lies on his or her back with legs parallel and arms to the sides. Relax into the floor.
3. B takes a position at A's right shoulder and manually stretches A's body. Place one hand underneath A's right scapula and the other hand on the chest area. Pull both hands simultaneously out and away from the center. Repeat on the left.
4. Take a position above A's head. Place both hands underneath A's upper back and gently stroke away from the center. Stay in contact with A's spine until the skull is gently released up and away. Repeat the action, but this time cradle the head in your hands and gently roll the head from side to side and forward and around. Continue extending the neck and head up and away.
5. Partner A needs to remain relaxed and trusting to release.
6. This exercise can be carried further with manipulation of the arms and legs by massaging and lifting up and away to release tension in the joints.

Exercise: Growing Taller

1. Stand with your feet six inches away from a wall, facing outward. Shift your weight back until only the back of the head is in contact with the wall. Maintain an upward energy flow. Stand in this position for one to two minutes.
2. Release to an upright position and walk away. What are your physical sensations and observations? How has your alignment adjusted?

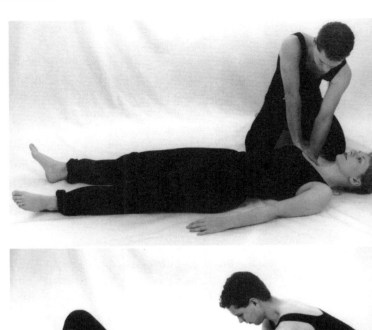

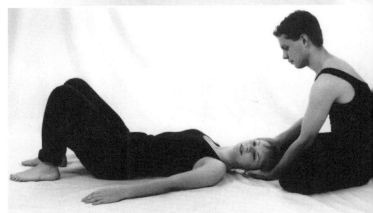

Exercise: Body Extension

Exercise: Sinking and Rising

1. Pair up with a partner. Partner A stands directly behind B.
2. Partner A places one hand firmly on each side of B's head. B bends the knees until the heels are almost released off the floor. A gently directs the head upward and B sinks down. Be gentle and firm. Do not use sudden movements or excessive force.
3. Once B is in a demi-plié position, A places one hand over another on top of B's head and provides gentle resistance as A rises to a straight leg position. Just as B reaches a full standing position, A releases the hands.

Explore each of these exercises to see if you can become more kinesthetically aware of a lengthened spine. Before and after each exercise, return to neutral and scan the body for unnecessary tension.

SUMMARY

It is essential that time and care be given to understanding your personal alignment. Your body is constantly adapting to new stimuli. What may feel natural is probably the result of years of habitual misuse. It is best to have a teacher help you discover how you can better use your body. If you are doing these exercises on your own work toward achieving a state of balanced neutrality by being sensitive to physical sensations and adjustments. With time, care, and effort, you will be able to work from a neutral position and create a character alignment that is based on information given in dialogue and action by a playwright.

JOURNAL ENTRIES

Describe or draw your alignment. What would you like to maintain and adjust? Why?

Where do you place your weight when standing? (Forward, backward, in the middle.) Are there any adjustments you would like or need to make?

When you shared your three-to-five-minute activity, did your alignment adjust to a different shape given the situation or circumstances changing? Describe your response and experience. Be specific.

Record additional observations, impressions, exercises, and ideas for future reference.

BREATH

Breath is the sustenance of life. It brings in needed oxygen, cleanses the blood, and reflects changing emotions. Breath is the origin of voice and movement processes. These are vital concerns for an actor.

Movement patterns reflect emotions, and changes in emotion alter breathing patterns. Breath is a response to mind-body connections. By observing yourself and others, you are able to notice breathing patterns in different situations. There are some generalities that may be made about breath and emotions: A person who is crying may take small, shallow breaths in a rapid tempo, while a person who is calm may take in long, deep breaths. There are many other examples of generalities to be made. However, it should be kept in mind that these are most often involuntary behaviors, and you should not attempt to control your breathing patterns during a moment-to-moment acting experience. Exploring breathing patterns can best be a resource for character and action development during classes and rehearsals. More importantly, optimal breathing patterns (ones that use full lung capacity) help to reduce tension and energize the body, mind, and spirit.

Because breath affects movement, an actor needs to be aware of breathing patterns and know how to use breath to facilitate movement. For instance, some people have a tendency to hold their breath or to take shallow breaths when performing repetitive movement patterns. This is because they are intimidated by the movement patterns and are subconsciously trying to protect themselves from making a mistake. Holding the breath is a result or symptom of the anxiety. This unfortunately makes matters worse by creating muscular tension because the muscles require oxygen to work effectively. An actor benefits from phrasing movement with breath.

Breathing is both an involuntary and voluntary activity. Altering breathing patterns demands concentration and heightened awareness. If you succeed in monitoring and using breath to your advantage with the following exercises, you will feel and see improvements in breath and movement connections.

BREATH: PERSON

Before you can begin to develop healthy breathing patterns and use breathing techniques for characterization, first acknowledge your personal breathing habits. The following exercises are designed to facilitate the study. Use these or other breathing exercises for an extended period to develop an accurate portrait of your breathing habits and patterns.

The terms "drop in" and "release" breath are used here instead of "inhale" and "exhale" because the latter set of terms implies forced breath control. The former terms are used by Kristin Linklater and are explained more fully in *Freeing the Natural Voice.*

Exercise: Breathing Habits

1. Lie on the floor with your arms and legs uncrossed.
2. Breathe in and release for five cycles. Aknowledge your normal breathing pattern rather than trying to create a more desirable one.
3. Place one hand on your abdomen and the other on your chest. Repeat five breath cycles. Notice if the breath seems to fill your chest and/or drop into your abdomen area.
4. Relax your hands at your sides and repeat five breath cycles.

At first it may be difficult to monitor your breathing. When thinking about how to breathe, the tendency is to alter the breathing pattern. With practice you will be able to eliminate this problem and be objective about your breathing patterns.

Repeat the above sequence in sitting, squatting, and standing positions. Notice any changes in your breathing patterns from one position to another.

Repeat the entire sequence with a partner. Observe each other in each position. Use touch around the middle and lower back to check for the amount of breath dropped in and released. Your objective is to let the maximum amount of breath flow in an out without strain and to support your movement. Share observations after both have completed the sequence.

Exercise: Varying Depths of Breath

1. While lying down, squatting, sitting, and standing, drop in just enough air to partially fill the lungs for five breath cycles.
2. Repeat and drop in a little more breath.
3. Repeat another five cycles, dropping in and releasing the maximum amount of air possible. Place your hands at the back of the lower ribs. Feel your lungs expand and the ribs move out from the sides. Let your abdomen release and move with the breath. Do not strain to pull in the air, rather let it flow into the torso.
4. Return to your preferred breathing pattern and feel how much air you drop in and release.

Exercise: Breath and Motion

1. Stand in neutral and acknowledge your breath pattern.
2. Walk around your working area, then pick up speed until you are running slowly. Notice what happens to your breathing.
3. Change the movement to skipping, leaping, galloping, and other locomotor movement. Continue to move until you are breathing rigorously. Be aware of your breath supporting the movement.
3. Slow down and stop. Tell someone a story, joke, monologue, or tongue-twister. Notice your breathing patterns and changes.
4. Keep talking until you return to a slow breathing pattern. Notice the amount of air you drop in and release to communicate.

Be aware of your breathing patterns based on physical and psychological expressions. Your breath will be natural and flowing deeply after vigorous movement if you are relaxed and not forcing the breath in and out. This is a natural breath pattern without restrictions because your body is responding to its needs. If there is a tightness in the abdomen or chest you are likely holding tension and not able to breathe at an optimal level.

BREATH: ACTOR

Maintaining your breathing habits at optimum levels provides support for demanding rehearsals and performances. Take in breaths that stretch your capacity, and be able to enhance the volume and release of breath as needed. Increase your observations and awareness of breath patterns as you link breath to emotions and vocal and physical behaviors simultaneously.

Begin with exercises designed to improve breathing habits. There is no single correct way to breathe, but the exercises are designed to improve your capacity and awareness. Like a singer or dancer who practices basic exercises regularly, practicing basic voice and body exercises routinely will lead to greater accessibility and responsiveness.

Exercise: Yawn and Stretch

Yawning is a natural function that draws in breath while the body stretches. It usually releases tension, allowing greater inhalation.

1. Stand in neutral and begin to stretch as if just waking up.
2. Let yourself yawn, stretch, and wiggle.
3. Settle into neutral.

Perform this exercise while standing and lying down. Roll about the floor as you stretch. Let sound be released. Be in touch with the richness of breath when it is deep and connected to a natural body function.

Exercise: Breath Flow

Breathing should be as little strained as possible. There are times when your breathing will be labored because of tension and exhaustion, but most of the time your breath should be without much effort.

1. Stand in neutral.
2. Close your eyes and concentrate on what is happening within you, not around you. Drop your jaw, relax the tongue on the floor of your mouth, and scan for unnecessary tension.
3. Breathe through your nose. Let the breath drop into your lungs and fill them to capacity, then release. Avoid creating extra tension in the chest or shoulders while breathing—remain relaxed.
4. Let the breath flow in and out and visualize the air as warm, light vapor streaming into your lungs, washing away the tension: Release and let go. You might also visualize the air as different elements. Use whatever helps achieve maximum capacity while still letting the air drop in and release.

Exercise: Breath and Emotion

1. Create a highly charged positive emotional event from your imagination. Let yourself become fully immersed in the details so that you are experiencing each moment. Visualize as many details as possible using all of your senses. What can you see, smell, taste, touch, and hear? Breathe and release the specific images. Let your breath respond with each sensation. Feel free to respond if you feel like smiling, laughing, sighing, etc.
2. Share your story with one person, and then another. After you have shared your story, immediately close your eyes and review your breathing patterns. Take a moment to process your thoughts, and be objective. Keep a notepad with you and jot down any relevant information about your breathing patterns and associated emotions.
3. Listen and be objective as the other actors tell their stories. Make mental notes about the connection between breath and emotions.
4. After everyone has told their stories, share what you observed and what you noticed about your own breathing patterns.

IMAGES

When using images in the following exercise the objective is to embody the essence of an object or idea. It is a process of identification, as opposed to imitation or indication. You are in search of the image's inner state. Ask yourself about the object's movement qualities, or being. You will concentrate on the qualities and embody them, first concentrating on breath, and then incorporating sound and movement. Because you are not seeking an imitation or indication but an identification, you will create an abstraction of the image. This frees you from a literal interpretation so you can make new discoveries. The intellectual process comes before and after the experience, not during. Before the process of identification, you will select an image's primal qualities, and after the experience you will objectively review your breathing patterns. During the experience give over to the image and let breath respond and support your movement.

Exercise: Breath and Images

1. Stand in neutral.
2. Drop in your breath and release until you feel the breath is fully engaged.
3. Think of a personal and positive image.
4. Describe the image's characteristics. Be descriptive. In a semi-audible voice, list the qualities. Narrow the list to three essential qualities.
5. Begin to concentrate on the image's primary quality.
6. Start your identification with the image through breath. Does the image inspire you to drop in deep languid breaths, or short shallow breaths, erratic breathing patterns, or light, fluid intakes and releases? Let yourself stay in contact with the image and bring it to life

through your breath. Release your feelings about the image through your breath. How does the image impact your experience, and how does this alter your breathing?

7. After experiencing the breath and image, return to a neutral stance and repeat at least five breath cycles to cleanse and refocus.
8. Repeat the steps above using a contrasting image.

Review how your breathing changed. Be specific. Let yourself get caught up in "I sense . . ." and connect your emotional and physical experience.

PHRASING BREATH WITH MOVEMENT

Phrasing breath with movement strengthens the connections among breath, action, and response. Breath connects the whole being to the activity and moment. Being able to phrase breath with sound and movement will also enable you to have enough breath for a phrase of dialogue or movement and to facilitate your actions as needed. Phrasing helps you to relax, gain confidence, and project energy. Learning to phrase breath with movements is extremely beneficial to actors who habitually hold their breath when approaching something they feel frightened about performing.

Exercise: Salute to the Sun

This yoga exercise is excellent for part of a generalized warm-up or cool-down, and makes the connection between breath and motion.

1. Stand in neutral.
2. Drop in breath as you place your hands palm to palm, and move them upward in front of your chest and face. Release the breath as you separate your hands up and out. Stretch from your torso from your hips.
3. Release forward and bend from the hips until you are hanging completely over. Let your entire spine release.
4. Drop in breath as you move into a lunge position. Stretch from your heel to your head.
5. Release breath as you move the bent leg back to parallel with the extended leg. Sit on your

heels with the torso and arms stretched out front.
6. Drop in breath as you scoop your chest along the floor until your body is stretched forward, supported by your hands and arms, with the head and spine arched.
7. Release the breath and lift the hips up and press the heels down in a jackknife position.
8. Drop in breath as you return to a lunge position (same as step 4, but on the opposite side).
9. Release breath as you bring the extended foot into parallel. Hang over from the hips, not the waist.
10. Drop in breath as you roll up through the spine.
11. Release breath in a neutral stance.

Exercise: Salute to the Sun

Exercise: Salute to the Sun

Exercise: Salute to the Sun

There are many exercises you can use to phrase breathing with movement. Be sure to alternate the intake and release with movements that are approximately equal in movement stress.

Exercise: Breath and Motion

1. Stand in a comfortable position and focus on your breath cycle.
2. Release unnecessary tension as the breath pattern becomes full and expansive.
3. Begin to move only on the release of breath. Phrase the movement with the breath.
4. Add movement on the intake of breath and suspend motion between the intake and release.
5. Add sound to the breath release. Let the movement reflect the breath and sound.

As you become more comfortable with phrasing breath and motion, play with the release of breath and sound. Sometimes you can release the sound slower, faster, stop and go, or move your tongue and lips to create new sounds and movement. Let movement and sound become harmonious. This is an excellent way to connect sound, movement, and breath.

SUMMARY

It is essential to acknowledge your own breathing habits, increase your breathing potential, and be able to unify breath, sound, and motion. Continue to use the breathing exercises as a part of your training process to help you relax, concentrate, and communicate.

Use breath to explore and release emotions, movement, and connections between breath and behavior. It is a valuable process when combined with knowledge of a character's needs, conflicts, and expectations in future studies.

JOURNAL ENTRIES

Describe the breathing pattern you are experiencing now.

What connection between breath and emotion did you make, or still have questions about?

Record additional observations, impressions, exercises, and ideas for future reference.

Describe an experience in which your breath changed with an emotion or action. Describe your physical and psychological responses.

CENTER

Unlike alignment, centering is a difficult concept to intellectualize because it cannot be seen when looking in a mirror but must be experienced from within the body. The center is where movement originates. The center begins motion with physical responses to stimuli, circumstances, emotions, and intellectual perceptions. The response begins with breath that connects to the center. Energy flows from the center and channels through the body to activate behavior. A person's primary center is determined by the individual's physical, mental, and intellectual characteristics. It is a result of physical and psychological history in addition to present circumstances.

The previous lessons, concepts, and exercises have provided a foundation for your observations and discoveries about your unique placement, alignment, and set of personal habits. At the same time, you can see that many people share some similar characteristics. You have a center that is unique to your body, but it may have some likeness with others. You can identify your personal center, locate a preferred center as an actor, and choose a character's center.

CENTER: PERSON

Your first goal is to identify your personal center. Allow yourself to be sensitive to movement impulses and origins.

Exercise: Locating Your Center

1. Stand with your eyes closed. Be aware of the space around you and how you fill space. Begin to move forward and take a step. Move slowly. Observe where the movement began. Take another step and reexamine. Repeat, breaking the action down moment by moment until you sense where the movement originated.
2. Give yourself an objective to take a step. Keep the same objective for several steps, and then select another. With each step and each objective, be sensitive to where the movement impulse began. Note: An objective is an acting term referring to a need and/or desire leading to action. Phrase your objective beginning with "I want/need to. . . . "
3. Do the same with sitting, running, skipping, and other activities.

Exercise: Observing Center During a Simple Activity

1. Observe yourself in a simple activity. This can be an everyday activity such as waking up, reading a newspaper, or making a cup of coffee. It is best to include larger movements such as moving from standing to sitting, walking, or using a large gesture so when you share the activity with an observer there will be a larger picture.
2. Pair up with a partner and recreate the activity. Be clear, and do not feel the need to "perform." Focus on your objective and action.
3. The observer will then describe the activity, movement qualities, and where the movement began—your center.

This exercise is just as valuable for the observer as for the one being observed. It takes a lot of time and practice to identify others' centers and habits. Once your observation skills are sharpened you will become more knowledgeable about movement and your own physical mannerisms.

The observer will look for areas of the body that appear to be initiating movement. The person doing the activity should only concentrate on the task and not on moving from an ideal center. It may take a series of self-observations and the help of others to determine where your center is located. Take time, and know that it may change as you change physically, mentally, and intellectually.

Physical changes such as weight gain, a minor injury, or a change in personal appearance more than likely will influence your self-image, possibly alignment, breath, and rhythms of movement, and all may affect where your movement originates.

When you feel depressed or on top of the world, your sense of unity, balance, and energy is altered. The mental changes you undergo may shift your center. The intellectual gains you make each day will also impact your perceptions of the world and your place within a community. With the new impressions come departures from past behavior based on knowledge and experience.

Once you feel you have located where a majority of your movements originate, you may want to examine why that is your primary center. Do this by examining past behavior. When did you start certain habitual gestures? Why? When did you begin walking with your current identifiable rhythm? Was there a change in your emotional or physical self-image? How do these relate to where your movement originates? Continually ask yourself questions to know who you are and why you behave the way you do. Do not get trapped by negative self-criticism, but rather heighten your awareness about your physicality and how you can utilize its maximum potential.

CENTER: ACTOR

There are several viewpoints about the nature and location of the ideal center. There is not a single ideal center for any actor in any given situation. You need to locate and nurture a center that enables you to focus your body, mind, and spirit in preparation for acting. In *To the Actor,* Michael Chekhov asks: "Imagine that within your chest there is a center from which flows the actual impulses for all your movements. Think of this imaginary center as a source of inner activity and power within your body." He adds: "So long as the center remains in the middle of your chest (pretend it is a few inches deep), you will feel that you are still yourself and in full command, only more energetically and harmoniously so, with your body approaching an 'ideal' type." Another ideal center is the solar plexus area. The definition of the solar plexus is: "1. The large network of sympathetic nerves

and ganglia located in the peritoneal cavity behind the stomach and having branching tracts that supply nerves to the abdominal viscera. 2. *Informal.* The pit of the stomach."

(*The American Heritage Dictionary of the English Language*)

The solar plexus is an ideal center because it is in the area near the belly where emotions are felt. The word "viscera" in the definition implies the link to strongly felt, or visceral, emotions. Dramatic action moves the story forward and the character's emotional reactions hold an audience's interest. The emotions felt deeply in the gut are strong and honest.

Some, including many martial artists, believe the ideal center is just below the navel and deep within the body. This area is the center of gravity that provides grounding and balance. In the article "T'ai Chi and Actor Training," included in *Movement for the Actor,* Linda Conaway writes: "All breath and movement begins in the tan tien'—that point in the lower abdomen right below the navel—and circulates throughout the entire body. This point is the reservoir of energy and center from which all movement stems."

Your definition of an ideal actor center may be different or the same as another actor's or director's. It is important that you find a sense of balance, harmony, and unity from within that can radiate throughout the body. Play with each of three centers: heart, solar plexus, and abdomen. Acknowledge the different sensations stirred through each center.

Exercise: Breathing and Centering

One of the best ways to center is through breathing. Your breathing reflects emotional changes, and often creates movement impulses. Try this exercise for each center.

1. Lie on your back.
2. Place your hands on the heart, solar plexus, or abdominal center. Focus on one center at a time.
3. Concentrate on the sounds you hear.
4. Let your concentration move from what you hear to what you feel, then back to what you hear.
5. Imagine that the center is being energized with warm air, and release tension. While working with the heart center, imagine filling

the lungs with air as if they were balloons, to full capacity without strain. Feel the chest expand and release. For the solar plexus center, imagine the breath flowing in like a light mist that tickles your solar plexus and is released with the exhale. Imagine the solar plexus area becoming warm and energized. For the abdomen, feel the breath stream down into the body, creating a gently swirling pool of liquid energy that will be a movement catalyst. If these images do not activate a response, discover ones that serve your movement preferences.

Exercise: Physical Stimulation of Center

During this exploration you will again awaken three different centers, but the focus will be on the use of physical stimulation. Many actors respond to the use of physical activation of a center more readily through actual contact or bold movements than through breath or imagery. Discover what works best for you.

1. Place your hands on your heart center. Breathe into the center.
2. Tap, stroke, or massage the area. Awaken the area through touch.
3. Activate the area through large movements. Let the chest move freely.
4. Create your own movements to physically awaken the chest center.

Contractions have long been used by modern dancers as a means of expression and control. They can improve sensitivity about your solar plexus center.

1. Lie on your back.
2. Let the breath drop in and release.
3. Contract the stomach area muscles by pulling them in and up toward the middle back. You might use the image of something hitting you in the stomach to sharpen the contraction. Hold the contraction for a few seconds, and then release and return to your natural breathing cycle.
4. Repeat the contraction and release. Locate the center.

Contractions may be repeated in several positions, including a seated position with the soles of the feet together or while standing. Because a contraction is a powerful action it should always be followed by a release. In addition, it is strongly advised that the entire body be fully warmed up before working with contractions, with particular attention paid to the spine.

Create your own movements to physically stimulate the solar plexus center. Move to a standing position when ready. Find large and bold movements to awaken the center.

The abdominal center is low and deep in the body. While it is in a typically heavier part of the body, it has all the mobility and focus afforded by the heart and solar plexus centers.

1. Lie down and place your hands on your abdomen and focus on the breath rolling down into the center with streams of warm energy.
2. With the soles of the feet planted firmly on the floor, roll the hips up and release down in a fluid motion. Make the movement small and slowly increase the range of motion. Initiate the movement from the pelvis.
3. Move to standing and circle the hips in large patterns. Feel the energized abdominal center activating the movement. Shift the hips forward and backward or in random directions. Let the movement awaken the center.
4. Create your own large movements to activate the center and its energy.

What impressions do you have about the differences of each center? Can you identify with one center more strongly than another?

Exercise: Centering with Images

1. Stand in neutral.
2. Let your breath drop in and out of a selected center.
3. Create an image of air or wind in your chest center, fire or sun within your solar plexus center, and water in your abdominal center. Play with one center at a time. Stay with the center as long as your interest is engaged, then move on to another center and image.
4. Let the image radiate energy from the center and move from the center.

What other images can you create where your center becomes an energy source and pulses energy out and away and back again? Create strong images.

When you lose a sense of being centered return to using images and breath. Start with slow and subtle physical activity. Gradually you will be able to take dynamic physical risks and maintain the sensation of being centered.

Exercise: Sound and Movement from Center

1. Stand, sit, or lie in a comfortable position. Breathe into the center of choice.
2. For the heart center, breathe in and release the sound "ay" as in play. Start off softly and, when ready, increase the volume, adjust the tempo, and play with pitch. Feel the vibrations of the sound radiating from the chest. Phrase the sound and breath with movement that begins in the chest center. The chest will lead in all your movements. Change the "ay" sound to "I love." The heart center in many cultures is associated with love and harmony. Experience the center from this point of awareness. When you are ready, complete a sentence beginning with "I love . . ." and let the words and movement harmonize. Don't force yourself to speak. Wait until you feel connected to the breath, sound, and action.
3. For the solar plexus center use the sound "ah" as in father and the verb "I can." Again, you will follow the same process by beginning with breath, using images, originating movement from center, releasing sound, and engaging words and phrases when ready.
4. The sound for the abdominal center is "oo" as in due. The verb associated with this center is "I feel." Follow the process used for the heart and solar plexus centers.

How did the sound activate the center? Did the centers have similar and/or different movement qualities? Which center did you prefer moving and sounding during this exercise?

Take elements from each exercise and combine them to create an intense experience for a selected center. For instance, if you choose to focus on the heart center: focus on breath releasing the area, physically activate the area with touch and large movements, use the image of air or wind radiating through the body from the heart, play with the sound "ay" coming from the heart, speak "I love" and initiate all movements from the heart/chest center. This can also be done for the solar plexus and abdominal centers.

Any one of these centers—heart, solar plexus, or abdominal—may be used depending on the character's needs, conflicts, and circumstances. The more comfortable you are with distinguishing each center, the more accessible the resources in creating a characterization will become.

SUMMARY

The identification of your personal center may be the most difficult part of this process. You will need to tune into subtle movements. Trust the vision of teachers and observers to help guide you toward a focused and centered physicalization. Resume study of your personal center after playing with the heart, solar plexus, and abdominal center exercises. You might have a greater sensitivity after the experiences.

Being centered during performance will be more accessible once you have opened up to the sensorial aspects of being centered. Tap into your movement preferences, whether it is use of breath, physical activity and exercises, imagery, or use of sound.

JOURNAL ENTRIES

Describe your primary personal center.

Describe the different sensations you experienced with the heart, solar plexus, or abdominal centers.

What approach works best for you to activate a center—breath, physical stimulation, imagery, or sound?

Process additional observations, impressions, exercises, and ideas for future reference.

SOUND AND MOVEMENT

The movement of breath over the vocal cords activates sound. Sound is composed of vibrations that stimulate movement within the body. The voice enhances movement and movement enhances the voice. Actor training that includes vocalization with movement supports the voice and body working together. However, simply engaging in sound and movement studies cannot replace the need to study each area separately. The energy produced through movement will enhance the voice by connecting breath to the activity. When passageways for vibrations are opened by breath both sound and movement are enriched.

The interplay of sound and movement is recommended for many exercises. Perform some of the exercises without sound, and then use the voice and note the difference. The sound will fill the body, engage the spirit, and assist in fully using the total self in communication. By activating the entire self you may discover many sound and movement possibilities previously unexplored. At first the discoveries offered by the experience may appear to be simple, but when invested with commitment a richness unfolds. You are not seeking to make the simple complex but to give yourself vital acting choices.

It would seem strange to prepare for a character by processing the vocal choices separately from the physicalization. The two work best when interlocked during the acting process. Let the voice support the body and the body support the voice. Be free to release sounds and movements you haven't previously experienced. Be adventurous! Take risks by letting the sound and movement release from your center.

The following exercises are not meant to be warm-ups. Give full attention to each area of the body during a warm-up in preparation for these exercises so your entire body will be ready to respond freely. Keep in mind that unnecessary tension may block a release of vocal and physical behaviors and prevent a full realization of communication potential.

SOUND AND MOVEMENT: PERSON

Begin with a personalized awareness of the breath and sound relationship. The changes in breath will influence sound. If the breath is full and connected, it will help release rich sounds, stimulating physical freedom.

Exercise: Breath and Sound

1. Lie down in a comfortable position on your back.
2. Let the breath drop in and release many times. Each time, the breath is full and deep.
3. When you feel the breath is released and connected, release a soft sound. The sound will be an impulse for movement. Allow the sound and movement to feed each other.
4. Send the breath to one part of the body. Simultaneously, release sound and move the area the breath embraced. Let the sound and movement complement one another.
5. Continue to direct the breath, sound, and movement through all areas of the body until the entire self has been awakened.
6. Repeat the above steps, and add images to bring additional energy to the work. Example: Imagine a warm spring day, and breathe the image into the right foot. On the release of the breath, stay connected to the image and let the sound and movement flow.
7. Repeat, connecting each part of the body with breath, sound, and movement while using images.

Exercise: Yawn and Motion

This exercise is much the same as the yawn and stretch exercise in the "Breath" chapter. However, the focus is now on awareness of the movement in relation to sound.

1. Yawn, stretch, and wiggle. These three movements are part of the natural physical response to awakening. Release sound with the motion.
2. Let yourself explore levels, directions, and range of movement. Feel the movement coming from deep within and experience its outward flow.

How does the simple, natural act of a yawn affect the physical response of the entire body? Did you sense the sound traveling through the body? Where did the sound and movement begin? Did you sense an awakening of the entire self?

Exercise: Sound and Movement from Center

1. Stand in neutral and connect breath to your center. Focus on the center becoming warm and bustling with energy.
2. With the breath, send a stream of energy to and from the center. The breath moves in not only through the nose and mouth but also seems to enter the body through all pores.
3. Direct the energy from the center to a specific area of the body. Let the area respond with sound and movement.
4. Add images to the breath and stream of energy. Keep the stream vivid and pure. The energy might be as powerful and forceful as a water cannon. The image may be the tingling glow of a laser light releasing and pouring out of the awakened area.
5. Do all of the above steps, but select a different center. Discover changes in the sound and movement based on where your center is located.

Were you able to connect the sound and movement to the image? Did the impulse begin from the center and travel outward to the specified area? Did you stop and intellectualize the connection, or let it flow? What images worked best for you?

During some of the following exercises you will share sound and movement. Keep the images strong yet adaptable. You may be influenced by another's sound and movement. Adjust with new impulses. Be flexible while maintaining the integrity of your images.

Exercise: Sound, Movement, and Color

1. Stand in neutral and connect breath to your center.
2. Visualize and breathe as a color. Sense the color flowing in with the breath and streaming into each limb and the torso. Imagine the blood and fluid in the body as color. Imagine the breath becoming a colorful mist as it is released. Release sound and movement. Imagine your body as a spray can of color. Select a part of the body to squeeze or contract and spray color. Imagine you can shake off color. Shake your head and color flies off the tips of your hair. Everything you touch becomes colorful. You can change colors. You are a living rainbow. The movement and sound are a reflection of the color traveling through your being. Stay connected to the color image.

How did one color impact your sound and movement in comparison to another color? What changes occurred in energy, breath, focus, and alignment? How did the energy or center change when you focused on a specific part of the body and activity?

SOUND AND MOVEMENT: ACTOR

Exercise: Sound and Movement with Partner

1. Face a partner and be sensitive to each other's breathing until both are breathing at the same rhythm.
2. When you feel connected to your partner, share a single sound and movement. Your partner will respond with a single sound and movement. Keep responding one at a time. Let it become conversational, without being literal, mimetic, or relying on conventional gestures to communicate. Just experience the sound and movement for what it is, not what it might represent.

What does it feel like to connect to another person's breathing rhythm? Did you wait for a need to communicate with sound and motion or did you force the gesture? Was the sound and movement connected? Did you hold back or release fully from your center?

Exercise: Sound and Movement Give and Take

1. Create a sound and movement phrase that is the essence of how you feel at this moment. Start by connecting your breath from your center. At a semi-audible level say "I feel" over and over. Your body will begin to transform with the breath. Let your body complete the phrase "I feel" with sound and movement. The phrase created should have a beginning, middle, and end. It is a statement of the self. It has form and shape.
2. Move through the space with the sound and movement phrase.
3. Acknowledge other people and their movement patterns. Transform to new sound and movement phrases as you are influenced by others.
4. Work new patterns and discover how they make you feel. Use your entire self.

What did you discover about your transformational movement phrases? What did you communicate? What did you sense about how other people were feeling through their sound and movement? What did you feel? What did you want? What did you need? Process your discoveries in your journal.

Exercise: Circle Game

This exercise has been adapted from games created by Joseph Chaikin and the Open Theatre.

1. All participants stand in a large circle.
2. One person moves to the center and creates a sound and movement phrase that is repeatable and adoptable by others. After clearly establishing the phrase, it is taken to another person. The phrase is shared until it is adopted. The two players exchange places.
3. The new leader takes the sound and movement phrase to the center and slowly transforms the sound and movement into a new phrase. This is taken to another person in the circle, and the cycle of exchange is repeated until all have participated.

This exercise is beneficial in trying new sound and movement phrases that you may not habitually select. It is also good for observation skills. But more importantly, it stimulates a means of sharing communication and transformation. Were you able to respond with the imagination and not with the intellect? Did you preplan your movements? What did you discover about yourself? What was the relationship of sound and movement in the transformation?

Exercise: Gossip Sound and Movement

1. All participants form a large circle.
2. One person shares a simple sound and movement with the person to the right. That person must fully imitate everything seen and heard and rapidly pass it to the next person.
3. Keep the sound and movement passing through the circle several times. Everything must be fully copied. This includes any deviations from the original sound and movement.

This is a variation on the verbal gossip game in which something is said and is passed as a secret through a group. The final statement is usually something quite different than the original. You can watch how sound and movement are interpreted and transformed as they move through an ensemble.

Exercise: Opposites in Sound and Movement

1. Start in neutral. Connect to your breath.
2. Create opposite qualities of voice and body. Begin with the breath. Allow it to begin to shape the physical. Transform to a physical quality that has a distinctive energy and pattern. Add sound that has an opposite quality. Examples: Create a soft lyrical movement pattern, then add a harsh jabbing sound; or create a jerky movement pattern and add a sustained sound quality.
3. Fully explore each opposite sound and movement phrase. Discover how it makes you feel. Interact. Let a relationship take shape. Stay in touch with the use of opposite qualities. Discover your needs, conflicts, and desires.

What persona emerged from your use of opposites? What qualities of sound and movement surfaced? How did working with another actor transform your sound and movement? Did you interact moment to moment? What was the shape of the relationship?

Discuss a movement response that was connected to sound.

SUMMARY

Using sound in the discovery of movement can be an enriching and rewarding experience. Stay open to new ways of moving and sounding, and to letting one invigorate the other. Even though these are not vocal exercises, you may be surprised at how they can open up sound and lead to stronger vocal choices in acting. The richness of sound will stimulate physical responses if you are sensitive to it traveling through the body. These exercises will help open up a variety of sound and movement qualities that may continue to grow and expand your acting skills.

JOURNAL ENTRIES

Describe your sensations when sound and movement were harmonious or dissonant.

Process additional observations, impressions, exercises, and ideas for future reference.

What types of sounds and movements do you favor? (high/low pitched, fast/slow, erratic/lyrical, big/small)

IMAGERY

Ideally, the mind and body are in harmonic union. The body is the communicating instrument for the mind. The most subtle images and thoughts will activate breathing patterns, connect to feelings, and influence physical behavior. Images have a strong physical impact because they often have an emotional power base. Sights, sounds, textures, smells, and previous taste experiences are mentally stored, and have corresponding recorded feelings associated with sensations. You can draw upon this resource as an information pool to stimulate images that complement a character's actions and responses. When the images are strong and are vividly engaged, they will impact the breath, alignment, tension, center, and energy.

An image of an object, person, idea, event, or animal can be personalized and expressed through behavior. The more powerful the image, the greater the psychological and physical response. What determines an image's power is personal, based on experience and knowledge. Experience has imprinted images in your mind and spirit. Visualization and sense memory can awaken the essence of experiences and transform behavior. When you do this in conjunction with acting it enriches the character and action because the moment is connected to spirit.

Be open and sensitive to an array of images and you will find ones that you can easily identify with and move you emotionally. What may be a powerful image for one person may not have significant relevance for another. When an image does not make a connection, move on to another. Discover the significance of images given by a playwright or director and personalize. If images are not given you are free to select ones that are appropriate to the character and that will release your imagination and physicality. Images are endless; seek the most powerful rather than the familiar, which might lead to a more stereotypical characterization. What may be more challenging is allowing yourself to dig deeply into your gut for a true response to the image rather than remaining in secure intellectual boundaries. Use the intellect to visualize the image and then let the visualization filter down into the foundation of your being. Let an electrical bond begin to flow between the visualization and the emotional release of the image. As the image is generated impulsively release movement and sound. Be vulnerable, honest, and sensitive. The exercises in this chapter will create a conduit through which revelations about imagery and essence can flow.

COLOR

Color images are often very powerful. A color can influence mood by stimulating sensory responses and passionate feelings. Color may be visualized with images, or you can work from responding to an external color you can see. While engaging in the following exercises stay focused on your personal response. If you are working in a group avoid getting caught up in the group reaction.

Exercise: Color

1. Select and visualize a specific color. It might help to picture a specific object that has the selected color in its composition. Focus on the color. Example: the color selected is bright red, and the representative object is a red bird.

2. Breathe in the color. With each inhalation let the color flow into parts of the body until the entire self is filled and is radiating the vibrancy and hue. Does the color stir a scent in your imagination, a sense of touch, a sound, a taste?

3. Release sound and motion with breath. The

air passing through your body is red. Red vibrates over the vocal cords and generates sound. What does your impression of red sound like? Feel the sound traveling through the body. Let the body move with the sound. Anything can happen. The only way to incorrectly sound and move is not to commit to the image and movement.

4. Beginning with one selected body area, toss the color through space. Paint walls, objects, and others with the color, shifting from one selected area to others. For example, the stream of color may first emanate from the fingertips, then from the elbows, then toes, and to any other physicality. Let sound flow with motion.

5. Acknowledge your breathing, focus, and energy as you radiate the color. How does it make you feel? What rhythms and moods are realized through sound and movement? Keep the connection flowing from your intellect to your spirit as you answer these questions. Stay focused on the color.

Do the exercise above with at least two other colors. Compare and contrast your responses. What sounds and movements were realized? How did they make you feel? What was your behavior? Record your responses in your journal.

After you have explored several colors select one for study and extend the exercise to include interaction with others using nonverbal sound and movement. Stay with the abstract and avoid mimetic or literal behavior. Respond to others by allowing yourself to physically and vocally modify behavior based on the stimuli.

SEASONS

Each season brings special recollections of people, events, situations, and feelings that are sometimes difficult to put into words. You may be able to express those emotions through movement, and from the movement release sounds and words.

Exercise: Image of Seasons

1. Lie on the floor with your arms at your sides and your legs uncrossed. Select a season. Be specific as to early or late in the season and the climate.

2. Breathe in sensations associated with the season.
3. What activities do you associate with the season? Let your breath respond to each image. Let yourself move with the breath. As the breath travels through the body let it impulsively stimulate sound. The sound is vibration. Let the vibrations transform into bold movements. Embody the season as you begin to move about the space.
4. Create a physical statement that communicates your feelings and connection to the season. The statement is a repeatable series of sounds and motions, like a thought or sentence communicated through the body and voice, that can be identified by others as having shape and form. When ready, share it with others.

Do the same steps in this exercise for two other seasons. Compare and contrast your responses. What character qualities emerged?

ESSENCE

Finding the essence of an object, action, music, or being is to discover the core that gives it an identifiable quality. Jean Sabatine describes essence studies in *Movement Training for the Stage and Screen* as "a primal, universal movement whose purpose is to allow the performer of the movement to embrace the totality of a living moment: its emotion, desire, and intention." It is experiencing the unique and universal aspects that creates shape, form, and life. It is stripping away the excess and being left with the essential. Sometimes this leads to abstract sound and motion that can be reshaped to conventional behaviors. Through this process an actor can have an experience that goes beyond intellect. It guides you to uncharted and unexplored territories of expression. By opening up new ways of thinking, moving, and sounding you find within yourself more freedom of expression, leading to greater virtuosity. This multifaceted point of view may be lying dormant within you. Societal conventions often repress the release of emotions and stifles behavior during adolescence. It may take time and effort to be able to fully express vulnerability in a new manner.

Essence work can be very stimulating and rewarding. It can open up new pathways of looking at the world and yourself. For the following exercise you need to study the object in detail, using all your senses to reach a new level of expression.

Exercise: Essence of a Balloon

1. Bounce a balloon with your hands, arms, chest, head, feet, back, and any other body part you can use. Focus on the balloon's movement. Does it spin, roll, or float? What are its movement qualities? Let the balloon bounce off the walls, floor, objects, and other people.
2. Watch the balloon descend through space and breathe with the balloon's motion. Begin to reflect the balloon's movement.
3. Let the balloon float away as you embody the balloon's essence. It is as if the balloon has floated inside you. You now have the balloon's qualities. Bounce, float, spin, etc.

Describe the experience of embodying the balloon's essence. What were the physical qualities? What were your emotional and physical associations? Record your responses in your journal.

Exercise: Essence of an Object

1. Select an object. Examples: an overstuffed chair, an electric fan, a tumbling mat, a chalkboard, or a piano. The overstuffed chair will be used for illustration purposes.
2. What are the object's qualities? Touch, smell, taste, listen, and see the object from every angle. As you explore the object with your senses, begin listing its qualities. For the chair, the qualities might be: soft, heavy, large, dusty, unkempt, abused, and lumpy.
3. Select three essential qualities of the object and embody one quality at a time through sound and movement. From the chair's qualities, you might use heavy, unkempt, and dusty. These tap into the senses of touch, sight, and smell.
4. Discover the essence of each quality, and physicalize with a simple movement statement. For example, focus on the chair's heaviness. Let your body become heavy. Your weight drops toward the earth's center. Your breath is coming from deep within, and responds to the burden. You lift your arm or take a step, but it is laborious. You move, but it is taxing. Even when you sit, lie down, or remain in a stationary position, it is with maximum effort.
5. Link the three physical statements into a move-ment study. Work this study while you focus on embodying the object's essence.

Keep the movement free and expressive. Anytime you feel the need to release sound, do so. The vibrations will enhance the movement. Be open to new ways of moving and sounding. Don't judge yourself during the process, but rather wait until the exercise is complete and then acknowledge your work.

The above exercise may be used for any object. Start with objects readily available rather than visualizing an object and trying to recall details. Be sure to explore the object with all your senses and verbalize qualities as they enter your thought process.

Once you feel secure discovering the essence of an object, explore others from your imagination or memory. Objects you might consider are ones from nature, domestic items, or personal mementos. For each item follow the same steps in the previous exercise, and always focus on the essential qualities.

ELEMENTS OF NATURE

Four primary elements of nature are earth, wind, fire, and water. During the Elizabethan period, these four elements were thought to correspond to the four bodily fluids: black bile, blood, yellow bile, and phlegm. An individual's physical and/or psychological imbalance was thought to be directly related to the imbalance of the bodily fluids. An imbalance stemmed from the dominance of one element. A corresponding temperament was associated with an element and bodily fluid. The earth element was associated with a melancholic personality, which was dominated by excessive black bile. If blood was the dominant bodily fluid then the person was thought to be sanguine, with wind being the corresponding natural element. Yellow bile controlled the choleric person, who was influenced by fire. A phlegmatic person was thought to have the dominant trait of phlegm, with water being the associated natural element. The "scientific" credence given to the elements, humors, and associated temperaments has an extensive history. Many references are made to these elements in the Renaissance plays. While the following exercise is helpful in character studies from period plays, it is also beneficial for other eras. Because you are using an image that is primary to existence, and because it is so complex, it has vast applications to the creative process.

Exercise: Essence of Nature's Elements

1. Visualize the element of fire. Use all of your senses.
2. Verbalize a list of qualities for fire (hot, dry, unpredictable).
3. Work through the following or a similar exploration of fire with sound and movement. Continue to visualize fire as you create its essence. Don't get caught up in a literal interpretation of presenting fire, but rather capture the spirit of the flames. You are a single flame licking the air. You are yellow and blue. You are hot. You are flickering. You are expanding to become more flames, like a campfire. You are erratic and unpredictable. Suck in air and use it as fuel. Burn and engulf anything in your path. Leap outside the campfire to light the ground and a tree. You are traveling and growing hotter. Your flames are larger. You are orange, yellow, and red. Engulf the trees. You are out of control and you destroy everything in your path. Feel a cool, gentle rain. Begin shrinking. You are blue and yellow. Sizzle as the rain cools your flames. Continue to flicker until the rain cools you to nothingness.

Do the same exercise for the elements of earth, wind, and air. Let your imagination be free to create associations for each element. Acknowledge the breath, energy, dynamics, and intensity you used to embody fire. What physical and emotional responses did you have during the exercise? What sound did you generate? How did the sound influence the movement and vice versa? What other images surfaced as you explored the fire's essence?

ANIMALS

Animal studies have long been a favored exploration. Humans readily identify with the nature of animals and use their qualities to describe man's behavior. Sayings such as "That person is a snake in the grass" or referring to someone as "gentle as a lamb" are commonly used to describe personalities. There are many more descriptions of human behavior and personality using animal qualities.

Use the following exercise identifying a character with animal behavior to find a prime focus in your study. Ideally, you will observe the animals in a natural or simulated setting, such as a farm or zoo. If you do not have access to live animals watch a video or look at pictures found in nature magazines or books.

Exercise: Essence Study of Animal Behavior

1. Lie in a comfortable position. Select an animal for essence study.
2. Visualize the animal in its natural habitat.
3. Talk to yourself as the animal, and describe your physical behavior and appearance. How do you sleep, eat, hunt, run, or stalk? Do you have feathers, scales, wings, or fur? Are you bipedal, or do you walk on four or more legs? Do you fly, swim, or crawl? List many characteristics.
4. Repeat the characteristics over and over. Breathe as the animal. Do you breathe through a nose, beak, gills, or mouth? Is your breathing shallow or deep? Let sound be released with the breath.
5. As you breathe, let your body begin taking on the animal's shape while at rest. Do you rest while lying down, sitting up, standing, or in suspended animation?
6. Open your eyes. Where do you focus? Do your eyes constantly shift? Do you stare at objects near or far? Do you meet others' eyes and hold contact?
7. Move and stay with the literal shape and focus as much as your body will permit. Do you move fast or slow? Do you slither, flit, bounce, roll, fly, dive, or lumber along? Be descriptive, and play it out through the body. Do not feel you have to constantly use locomotive activity: You may come to a stationary position if the animal you have embodied would do so.
8. From head to toe, examine each body part for movement qualities. How do you hold your head? What is the length of your neck, and how does it move? What is your torso, chest, or body like? Do you have a spine? If so, how is it formed? Do you have arms, wings, or fins? How do they move? Where are your major joints and what is their range of motion? Do you have legs? How many? Go over every section of the body and create detailed movement.
9. Build your habitat around you. What do you

see, feel, taste, smell, and hear? Be specific. Play and work within your habitat. Make it your own. Go through typical behavior.

10. Interact with other animals.

11. Pull away from the others and resume a resting position. Focus on the animal's primary behavioral characteristics. What are the animal's essential physical and behavioral qualities? Focus on those traits, and slowly transform your animal behavior into more essential behaviors. Be economical.

12. Translate the animal's behaviors into human behavior.

13. Stand, sit, lie down, walk, run, and gesture as a human with the animal's essence. Focus on your alignment, placement, energy, focus, breath, and rhythm of human behavior using animal qualities.

What animal did you select? Why? What movement qualities and behavior did you discover as the animal? How did you transform the animal's physicalization into human form? What were characteristics that you found within yourself using the animal's essence?

MUSIC

Almost everyone at one time or another has heard a song and been instantly transported to another time and place because of the emotions, memories, and images stirred by the music. It is often a powerful and yet subtle reaction that touches your breath, energy, and impulse for action. It is more than emotional recall. It is a state of being that is associated with the music. It might be a specific memory of a person, place, time, or event that flashes in your mind when you hear the music. It might be a season, period of life, community, or a fantasy world that is evoked. Whatever the origin, it is personal and very rich.

It is rich because music has an immense depth in relation to emotions and physical responses. Individual responses to lyrics and melody are as vast and varied as the musical spectrum itself. For example, one selection may stir your intellect with the lyric, while another piece may have a melody line that can bring a buried emotion to the surface. Some songs may have equally powerful lyrics and melody lines that capture the spirit and extend the range of psychological and physical responses.

Movement for actors and movement for dance should not be confused. Dance is composed of movement patterns often choreographed to musical phrases and rarely uses vocalization. Movement for actors, on the other hand, typically is not set to music and often utilizes the voice. Be aware of this difference so you are not limited to dance phrases when using music for a movement stimulus. Instead, the music should free you to focus on the emotional response and release through the body and voice. Harness the inspiration that music gives and channel it into your movement. Because music can have such an instantaneous response, do not predict behavior but rather let it happen with the moment.

For each of these exercises, begin in a balanced state, both mentally and physically. Work from an abstract point of view about the music rather than attempting to physicalize the literal meaning of the words or rhythms. It is best to avoid working with music with lyrics until you are comfortable working from the melody alone. Incorporate all of your senses with the music. First listen and visualize. Let the music awaken all your senses, and feel it move through your body, mind, and spirit.

Exercise: Music and You

1. Listen to a piece of music. Breathe in the music, and open up all your senses to its inspiration. Be open to images and emotions that the music evokes. Let your breath release the experience.

2. When ready, let the body respond with sound and movement. Move on impulse: Avoid preplanned dance movements. Let the music move you. Feel that your body is conducting the music. Become one with the music, so it is difficult to tell whether the music is leading you or you are leading the music.

Were you able to let yourself go with the moment and the music's essence? Did you spontaneously respond without preplanning what might look good or feel right? What did you discover about yourself and your response to the music? Record your responses in your journal.

Repeat the previous exercise, but use a medley of music. Impulsively respond to the musical changes. Find different attitudes and interpretations through movement. Discover new ways of moving that come from the music. Tap into emotional responses to the music and movement, and release vocally and physically.

How did your physicality change with the music? When the music changed did you stop and intellectualize your next movement? Were you able to let your emotions flow with the music? What images, ideas, and feelings surfaced? Record your responses in your journal entries.

Exercise: The Essence of an Instrument

1. In a comfortable position, listen to a piece of music.
2. Focus your attention on the sound of a single instrument. Listen to its line and harmony, tempos, accents, and rhythm. When does it become loud or soft?
3. Play the music again. This time, embody the instrument's essence.
4. Move with and react to the others around you, who are also playing their bodies as musical instruments within the composition. Create an ensemble.

What did you find in the relationship with others? How did you embody the instrument? How did you work together as an ensemble in creating the musical composition? How did your movement and interpretation contrast or harmonize with those around you? What did you discover about your contribution to the piece as a whole through the instrument's essence? How does this relate to acting?

Exercise: Song of the Body

1. In comfortable standing position, recall a musical selection and play it in your head.
2. Breathe with the recollection and begin to softly hum. Let the vibrations travel through the body.
3. Play the song through the body. Interpret the essence of how the song makes you feel. What does it make you want to do? How does it carry your body through space?
4. Allow the hum to transform into random sound, but continue the movement. Capture the song's essence by how it inspires you to move and sound.
5. Share your feelings, sound, and movement with others. Let them feel the music's essence through you.

Why did you select that particular song? What emotions did it arouse? How did your body move with the music? What did you discover about yourself?

NONMUSICAL SOUNDS

Nonmusical sounds often have a strong emotional impact just as music does. These are sounds that do not have a set rhythm or composition and are heard randomly. Some sounds, such as rain patter on the roof, leaves rustling down the street, or birds chirping in the morning, may not be classified as music but may have musical elements. Sounds such as a baby crying, a doorbell ringing, car tires squealing, or a dog barking may set off an emotional reaction that may or may not have ties to a past experience. You encounter a variety of sounds each day. Many of the sounds you have trained yourself to block out or react to minimally. Other sounds trigger an immediate response and touch raw nerves. Be sensitive to your reactions to sound, and channel into the acting process.

Exercise: Nonmusical Sounds

1. Start in a comfortable position.
2. Using live or taped sound effects, react to the sounds you hear with sound and movement. Breathe in the sound's essence and react on impulse. Choose not to preplan your reactions or stop to think of how you should react.

What discoveries did you make about your reaction to the various sounds? What sounds seemed to bring forth the most violent reactions? Which sounds seemed to stir the most peaceful reactions? Did you have any emotional flashbacks or recall specific moments in your life? How did the sound affect your emotions, mood, and attitude? How did they affect your physical and vocal behavior?

EVENTS

Major holidays and events in your life imprint images and memories in your mind. Just the mention of the Fourth of July, graduation, a wedding, or a special event may heighten emotions and influence physicality.

Exercise: Essence and Events

1. Start in a comfortable position. Select an event for essence study. Birthdays will be used as an example.
2. Verbalize what birthdays mean for you.
3. Create the essence of the impressions and descriptions through sound and movement.
4. Form a simple sound and movement phrase. Physically state the essence of what birthdays mean to you.
5. Share with others.

Repeat the exercise using major holidays, special occasions, or events that are easy for you to recall in detail. What did you discover through the movement phrase about your feelings for the event? What impressions did others receive when you shared the movement phrase?

How did you use a season's image or an element of nature to find movement and acting impulses?

Describe physical and psychological changes you experienced during the animal studies.

SUMMARY

Imagery studies are exciting because the possible choices for study are endless. Any idea, object, animal, music composition, or element of nature may be used. In some cases, using a contrasting image may be of value for discovering character traits that you may have thought inappropriate. Moving in a new direction and pattern may open up exciting aspects of behavior and action choices.

Work with powerful images to discover exciting choices. As an actor you create images for the audience. To stir their imagination, you must be fully connected to a dynamic idea through your body, mind, and spirit. You can do this by physicalizing a specific and powerful image. Ideas locked in the intellect will not be experienced by the spirit and released through the body.

What physical and psychological connections did you make between music and movement?

Record additional observations, impressions, exercises, and ideas for future reference.

JOURNAL ENTRIES

What color or colors do you find easier to visualize and release through sound and movement? Compare or contrast several colors and physical behaviors.

SPACE, TIME, WEIGHT, AND ACTION

Rudolf Laban (1879–1958) was a choreographer, scientist, artist, and movement educator who developed a movement system known as Laban Movement Analysis (LMA). Laban spent years observing movements of people engaged in domestic and professional activities. His observations created a movement vocabulary used to define behavior. Many factors are part of LMA and are worth investigation. The ones outlined in this chapter are space, time, weight, and action. These are essential factors that represent a very small portion of Laban's theories. The actor's study of the quantitative and qualitative applications of space, time, and weight can provide a primary foundation for movement vocabulary.

The applications of Laban's theories of space, time, and weight have tremendous acting value because Laban defined the movement factors with qualitative attitudes. The attitude is that part of a person's inner state that is influenced by environment, situation, and circumstances. The inner drive toward movement has been translated as Effort. Effort studies can be a basis for acting explorations that will eventually lead to characterization choices.

The terminology used to describe quantitative space, time, and weight values is common dance and music vocabulary. They are external and include direction, level, range of motion, rhythm, tempo, meter, accent, rest, dynamics, and intensity. These explorations will help you develop a better understanding of your personal movement potential, your affinities as an actor, and various pathways available for creating a character and accessing expressive behavior.

QUALITATIVE SPACE

Laban defined two attention factors for space: direct and indirect effort. The attention factor refers to the attitude toward spatial awareness, i.e., how you attend to the space. If you have a singular or narrow focus, you are using direct space. The direct space effort utilizes a concentrated and linear perception.

The indirect space factor is defined by a multiple focus. When you are engaged in the indirect space effort your attention to the space and environment absorbs many stimuli with variable awareness levels. Attending the space with an indirect inner drive will likely give you the sensation of taking in the entire environment. Another translation for Laban's term for the indirect space effort is "flexible." This implies an easy shift from one environmental factor to another.

As you heighten your awareness of direct and indirect attention to space, remind yourself that you are exploring an attitude and physical experience. Discover or create an objective and action as you move. Open your imagination to suggestions made by and through the motion.

Exercise: Direct and Indirect Space

1. Imagine that you are at a market. You have an idea about what you have come to buy, but are just as interested in "shopping around" for bargains. Let your attention wander through the environment; take in the smells, sights, sounds, textures, and tastes. You are able to absorb many sensations.
2. A particular sound captures your attention. Tune in and listen. What do you hear? Where is the sound coming from? Follow the sound. Investigate. Pinpoint its origin.
3. Once you have found the sound and your curiosity has been satisfied, return to exploring the many features of the marketplace. Fluctuate between a narrow focus on a special point of interest—a sound, taste, texture, etc.—and back to attending multiple points of interest.

When was your direct and indirect spatial awareness heightened? Describe the psychological and physical experience.

Exercise: Movement Score Using Direct and Indirect Space

1. Design a short movement score where the activity involves coming into a room to find something, locating it, and leaving.
2. Work through the piece several times with a heightened awareness of when indirect and direct spatial intent is heightened.
3. Make movement choices and economize the activity, and prepare to show the score to others. Be clear about your objective and given circumstances.
4. Share the score with others and discuss observations.

Exercise: Direct and Indirect Space During a Conversation

1. Discuss a subject of interest with a partner. Let yourself be involved with the other and the conversation.
2. Heighten your spatial awareness. When do you use a narrow band of attention, and when does your focus shift to various stimuli?

Discuss spatial awareness observations and the shifts in attitude and behavior.

QUANTITATIVE SPACE

Space is easy to identify since it surrounds you. Space can stimulate all your senses. Most likely you have different responses to being in a large open space or a confined space. Most responses to space are influenced by given circumstances. One of the keys to your investigations is to stay open and vulnerable to sensations. You move through space and sense how it changes because you have altered your place and shape within it. Space is continually being reshaped because of your movement. You may feel that you have more direct control over space than time and weight because you inhabit space and can move objects about within it. Explore the basic quantitative space components: direction, levels,

and range of motion. Give yourself actions and/or objectives to motivate the movement explorations as needed.

DIRECTION

Direction refers to your position in relationship to a fixed point. When you change direction you alter your position to the specified fixed point. You can move in numerous directions, including forward, backward, sideways, and on a diagonal plane.

Exercise: Changing Directions

1. Select a reference point and change directions. Walk toward the point, away, on a diagonal, in profile, and in other directions.
2. Note how the space is shaped and how your relationship to the fixed point is altered by the movement's direction.
3. Repeat, but use a person as your reference point. Note changes in the relationship. Discuss your impressions and observations.

LEVELS

Level changes occur when you alter your position in space, either up or down. The use of levels can suggest power, weakness, self-esteem, aggressive or submissive behavior, and a host of other connotations. Many people are accustomed to speaking and relating with others on the same level or at conventionally differing levels, such as one person sitting and the other standing. Use of levels can illustrate conflict and define character and relationships.

Exercise: Levels

1. Explore moving on low planes by slithering, crawling, scooting, and walking with a bent-over shape. Explore many ways of moving on a low level. Add sound.
2. Explore various levels between bent-over and upright. Move toward objects, sit, stand, and run.
3. Explore levels above upright. Walk on your toes, jump, and climb.
4. Mix all levels and include rolls, falls, jumps, skips, glides, etc.

5. Relate to others using different levels. Let relationships and characters evolve. Use nonverbal sound.

What did you sense when moving on the lowest level? How was this different from the upright level? Was the sound influenced by the physical behavior? What happened as you interacted with others and incorporated various levels? Record your impressions in the journal.

RANGE OF MOTION

Range of motion is governed by the expansion or contraction of part of the body. Range of motion is the degree of physical extension from center. A gesture's range is more than how far the arms and hands move in and away from the torso. You can also move your torso toward and away from center through contraction and expansion movements. You can gesture with your legs, shoulders, and head. All of these areas have a range of motion that contribute to defining emotions and action behaviors. Your range of motion may be larger or smaller than you consciously perceive. Stay open to new experiences and observations.

Exercise: Range of Motion

1. Explore the range of motion of arms, legs, head, and torso by creating gestures that reach out and pull in at varying degrees. Select objectives and actions such as to locate, to obtain, to dislodge, to affix, etc. Start in a stationary position. Take your time to find new movements.
2. Move across the floor in different directions and use various levels while you explore range of motion using just your arms. Then use just your legs, then head, then torso.
3. Intermix gestures from all parts of the body as you move through space. Use the entire body to communicate. Add sound but not words.
4. Interact with others. Work with one or two body parts at a time. Switch to using other body parts on impulse.

You are now prepared to heighten your spatial awareness by experiencing how space fills and shapes the body and how the body fills and shapes space. As you expand your internal spatial awareness in the next exercise connect to external space. Freely employ the components of direction, level, and range of motion.

Exercise: Space Within

1. Lie on your back with the arms and hands at the sides and the legs extended. Close your eyes and go on a journey inside your body.
2. Let the breath drop in and fill the lungs. Sense the breath's movement in the lungs. Trace the breath and be aware of spatial changes within the chest area. Mentally measure the distance from front to back and side to side. Heighten your sense of the entire chest from the inside. Sense the chest's outside boundaries and how they define space.
3. Let the breath pour into the right leg. Follow the breath and feel the space within your foot, calf, knee, and thigh. Sense the distance inside the body from the toes to the pelvic area. Let your awareness move to the leg's outside dimensions and occupied space.
4. Work through steps two and three for each body part. Be aware of the internal and external space that the body part defines.

Exercise: Nonlocomotor Movement Through Space

1. Imagine moving the right arm from the shoulder. Visualize it lifting and gliding about yourself before laying it back down at your side. Visualize how the arm cuts through space.
2. Open your eyes and lift the right arm from the shoulder. Watch how it moves through space and alters its basic relationship to the body. Move the arm in all directions, varying tempos, levels, and range of motion before returning it to a restful position.
3. Repeat the same basic action premise for the legs and head. A reminder: Add the use of actions and/or objectives if this helps you connect the physical and psychological responses.
4. After each major body area has moved, move more than one area at a time while remaining stationary. Be sensitive to how the space changes.

Exercise: Exploring Space with Locomotor Activity

It is beneficial to perform this exercise immediately following the previous one, and allow the body to begin slowly moving through space.

1. Move through space, include sitting, standing, walking, running, and jumping. Start very slowly so you can feel the changing nuances of space. Sense your relationship to other people and objects. How is your sense of space condensed and expanded?
2. Select objects or other people that you move toward and away from. Be aware of how your perception of the space is altered.
3. Become conscious of perceptual changes as you change levels, directions, shapes, and designs in space. As you move through space sense how it is redefined.

Exercise: Sustain and Go

1. Move slowly through space. Let your body be free to find new designs.
2. Without preplanning, create and sustain a position. Experience how you fill the space. Is there an emotional or psychological response to the shape and design? Let it go and move on. Sustain motion and move on impulse.

Exercise: Moving Around Another

1. Pair up with a partner and move around each other, noticing how your relationship changes because the space between you is altered. Avoid contact during early explorations.
2. Move about the other person adding physical contact. Note how the relationship changes. Focus on shaping space together.
3. Add an object as a focal point, and move around it. (Examples: sofa, chair, desk). Allow contact with the object and each other to happen on impulse.

Exercise: Exploring Various Spaces

1. Explore different rooms and the outdoors. Experience each as a new space. Physically respond to the space's size, shape, volume, and atmosphere.

2. Examine how your sense of space is altered. How did your physical and psychological behavior adjust to the new space? Did you harmonize with or try to dominate and control the space? Continue asking yourself questions and heighten your perceptions.

Exercise: Theatre Spatial Awareness

1. In a theatre space where the audience area and performance space is defined, start in a stationary position. Focus on harmonizing with the space by radiating energy in all directions. Be aware of the space above, below, front, back, and to the sides. Fill the space with your energy.
2. Move through the space and feel how you shape the performance area, and how your spatial relationship to the audience adjusts. Explore all areas of the performance space.
3. Explore various levels, directions, shapes, and designs. Be aware of how the space is altered by your movements.

SPATIAL RELATIONSHIPS

Exercise: Sharing the Space

1. Face a partner within touching distance.
2. Connect to the other's breathing.
3. Feel the floor. Listen to the sounds. Smell the air. Look out through space and sense that you are a part of it, and include your partner.
4. Look into your partner's eyes and make the choice to embrace and share the space.
5. Back away a few feet and continue to share the space. Continue backing away. Walk about the space and continue to communicate with your partner through spatial usage.

A basic acting principle is to actively embrace the other's presence. It seems obvious, yet many actors feel alone onstage because this primary communication line has not been fully opened.

Exercise: Form and Relationship

1. One person goes to the playing space, takes any form, and maintains the shape's integrity. Others observe what the shape suggests.

2. One person joins the other and creates a new shape and relationship. Sense how a relationship is established by reshaping the space.
3. After a shape and relationship has formed, one actor changes the use of level, direction, or range of motion.

Discuss the relationship created. How did changing the use of space alter the relationship? This exercise may be expanded by adding a third person. It is best to limit it to two actors at first so the observers and actors have the opportunity to start with a more simple composition.

Exercise: Interaction in Space

1. Pair up with another actor. Begin in neutral and focus on the other.
2. When you both sense an open communication line begin moving from stationary positions to shapes and back to suspended motion. Spontaneously respond to each other. You are not mirroring each other but exploring spatial relationships. Keep your mind open and avoid thinking about what movements you will do next.
3. Explore the use of levels, directions, and range of motion.
4. Let sound be released on impulse.
5. Let a situation evolve. Add single words or short phrases. Stay focused on your spatial relationship.

How did spatial awareness help shape the relationship? Did the use of distance, level, direction, or range of motion influence your connection to your partner? If you observed the exercise, describe the action and its impact.

QUALITATIVE TIME

While time and space can be measured by clocks and dimensions, time seems less tangible because its value is often subjective. What may seem like a long time period for one person may feel like a fleeting moment for another. A minute can be measured as sixty seconds but is perceived differently by individuals based on immediate needs and situations.

The time effort factors are defined by the attitude toward time. One factor is "quick" and the other is "sustained." When the quick time effort is active there is a sense of urgency. The pulse rate may seem faster. Ideas and impulses move suddenly. In contrast, when responding with sustained effort the tendency is to linger and suspend time. There is an endlessness to activity. You may feel you can indulge in time and sustain a moment.

Exercise: Quick and Sustained Time Explorations

1. Imagine that you have been asleep. Awaken and get ready for the day. You wake up early and have plenty of time to do your morning rituals like dressing, eating, reading the paper, etc. Begin your activities with a sustained time attitude.
2. About midway into your morning ritual you look at the clock and see that you are running very late. Shift to a quick time effort as you finish your morning preparations. Reminder: Select an objective and given circumstances.

Exercise: Time Movement Score

1. Create a short movement score that involves at least one dynamic shift in the time effort and then show it to others for observation and discussion. Example: Come into a room searching for something specific. You need the item immediately and the quick time effort is dominant. You must make decisions concerning where to look for the misplaced item. Search. You find the item and the time effort changes to sustained. Create a conclusion.

Discuss how the movement quality changed when the time factor changed. What did you feel happening psychologically and physically? What did others observe?

QUANTITATIVE TIME

Time values and terminology that musicians use are also applicable for an actor. Explore the use of tempo, meter, rhythm, accent, and rests. While your focus will be on the external application of time, you will likely experience an internal response.

Exercise: Tempo

Tempo is the rate of speed (fast/slow) during an activity.

1. Perform a simple activity such as walking from one point to another and explore various tempos. Give yourself actions such as to pursue, to stalk, to linger, etc.
2. Perform a simple gesture. Repeat, but vary the rate of speed. Continue repeating the gesture using different tempos.

What response did you have while performing the activities and gestures at different speeds? Identify connections between how you physically move and how you psychologically or emotionally respond.

Exercise: Meter

Meter is the repetition of movements or sounds at regular intervals that mark the passage of time. It is unlikely that you will consciously perform a character's activities to a fixed meter unless you are in a musical. However, exploring a meter's essence may be informative about your personal choices and for a character's preferences.

1. Select a piece of recorded music. Listen and begin to physicalize the meter. Start with 4/4 or 3/4 meter.
2. As you move about the space allow anything to happen. Explore the space using different levels, directions, and range of motion.
3. Begin moving in everyday patterns while staying true to the meter. Do not use dance patterns.
4. Stop the music, but continue to move with the meter's essence.
5. Select another piece of music with a different meter, and repeat steps one through four. Acknowledge how this differs from the previous meter in physical and psychological responses.

Exercise: Rhythm

Rhythm is the meter set to repeatable patterns at regular or irregular intervals. Think of rhythm as being the essence of the notes floating within the framework of the meter. In this context, the notes (actions) have structure that may be defined in repeatable patterns at regular or irregular intervals.

1. Listen to a piece of music and let your body respond to the rhythms. Feel the emotion and style of the music. Let it flow through your body.
2. Move through space as you physicalize the essence of the music's rhythm.
3. Move in everyday patterns such as sitting, walking, standing, and gesturing while keeping the rhythm's essence.

Exercise: Accent

Accent is the stressed movement or sounds within a phrase that typically marks the beginning.

1. Create a movement sequence.
2. Repeat the sequence many times and focus on using accents to highlight specific movements.

How does the movement sequence take a more defined shape based on use of accents? How did changes of accent alter the expression of ideas?

Exercise: Rests

A rest is a moment of stillness and quiet. It has the same quality as a pause. Some very theatrical and enlightening moments in theatre occur during pauses. The action still has a strong focus, but for a moment dialogue and activity are suspended.

1. Move through space and come to rest on impulse. Keep alternating motion with stillness.
2. Work with levels, directions, range of motion, tempo, meter, rhythm, and accents. Let anything happen. Explore and be free to move without the need to watch yourself.

QUALITATIVE WEIGHT

When you make a choice and begin a course of action, you have an intention. The inner attitude behind your intention may be strong or light. These are the two weight effort factors. When you are strong you are "putting your weight" behind the intention.

Your attitude will be firm and you may have a sensation of heaviness. A strong effort is associated with being aggressive or assertive and incorporates a degree of resistance. A light weight effort creates the sensation of gentleness and levity. It is a yielding or indulging element. A light weight may be associated with a passive attitude and behavior.

Exercise: Strong and Light Weight

1. Imagine that you have a problem to solve. You have solved similar problems before and enjoyed the challenge. Work with a light effort and physicalize.
2. You have a second problem to solve that requires a strong weight effort. It is a more difficult problem, one that you believe you can solve but requires a forceful commitment. Be assertive or aggressive. Your intention is firm.

What was the psychological and physical difference between solving the problem with strong and light weight? How did your behavior change?

Exercise: Weight and Intention

1. Tell a short story to a group. What is your intention? To impress, to entertain, to insult, etc.?
2. Make a choice to begin with strong or light weight. Use your entire body during the storytelling. As you tell the story the weight factor may change.
3. Discuss with the group what weight effort they observed and what you sensed during the storytelling experience.

QUANTITATIVE WEIGHT

While you cannot change your quantitative body weight at will, you can change your physical weight experience. You can feel heavier and lighter through physical and perceptive adjustments. Many people commonly do this on a subconscious level. A person may feel physically heavier or lighter even though the actual weight is unchanged. The varied weight sensation may be accompanied by a psychological adjustment. You can explore adjusting your quantitative weight sensation and observe how the physical and psychological be-

havior is modified. From the exploration, discovery, and observation processes you can integrate character and action choices during a rehearsal process.

Exercise: Heavy Weight

1. Visualize yourself becoming physically heavier.
2. Breathe into the feet, legs, pelvis, torso, arms, and head and visualize that they are filled with sand, clay, or water.
3. Physically allow your muscles to soften and collapse. The ribs may collapse, but do not actively pull the ribs in toward center. Imagine that your body is dense matter.
4. Fill the space with your physical presence. Perform an everyday activity with a heavy weight sensation. What is your experience? Has your sense of time and space been adjusted? Do you have a different sense of self? What is your physical and psychological experience?

Exercise: Light Weight

1. Use the same process as in the previous exercise but substitute lighter images like air, clouds, feathers, etc.
2. When you adjust the physicality release the joints: Allow the chest to expand, the legs to drop away from the pelvis, and the head to float.
3. Perform a daily activity. Note the physical and psychological behavioral preferences. Is there any difference from when you incorporated a heavy weight sensation?

ACTION

Balanced combinations of space, time, and weight efforts create what Laban identified as Basic Effort Actions. There are eight Basic Effort Actions also referred to as Action Drives: float, punch, glide, slash, dab, wring, flick, and press. These actions offer the actor solid connections to psychological and physical behaviors that may serve as acting choices. As you explore an action give equal weight to each space, time, and weight effort within the combination. During the explorations you may want to add objectives and/or actions that seem appropriate.

Punch is a combination of strong weight, direct space, and quick time. Punch an imaginary object with your fists. Breathe with the motion. Move the action through your body into your legs and punch with your feet. This may result in kicking, stomping, or similar movements. Stay with strong weight, direct space, and quick time as you activate other body areas. Keep the entire body responsive. Connect your physical activity with psychological attitude. Continue exploring punch and tell a nursery rhyme or poem, or improvise dialogue.

Press is a combination of strong weight, direct space, and sustained time. Press against a wall, floor, or solid object. Use your hands, feet, and back. Move away from the structure and press against an imaginary object with your elbows, head, and other body areas until your entire body has explored the press action. Select an objective and use press as your action as you perform an activity. Add words. Again, you might use a nursery rhyme or poem and be aware of how the delivery changes with a different action.

Slash is a combination of strong weight, indirect space, and quick time. Slash through an imaginary overgrown jungle. Use all parts of your body to make your way. Go beyond conventional behaviors. This may mean changing levels and directions and varying the range of motion. Connect external and internal behaviors. Add words or text.

Wring is a combination of strong weight, indirect space, and sustained time. Wring out an imaginary soaking towel. Use the arms, torso, and legs. Breathe with the movement. Release sound. Imagine your body is a wet towel and wring your body. You might begin with wringing one leg and then both, then the torso, and then various body areas. The movements can range from large to small. Play and discover. Let your attitude reflect the strong weight intention, indirect spatial attention, and the sustained time effort. Add words.

Dab is a combination of light weight, direct space, and quick time. Pick up an imaginary paintbrush and dab paint on a canvas, or create another imaginary situation. What is your attitude when using the dabbing action? Add sounds and words.

Glide is a combination of light weight, direct space, and sustained time. Explore activities that typically use gliding actions such as ironing, ice skating, shaving, stroking a pet, or raking leaves. Any of these activities may be done with various intensities of light weight, direct space, and sustained weight. Reminder: Maintain an equal balance of the efforts.

Flick is a combination of light weight, indirect space, and quick time. Flick away imaginary confetti off yourself. Flick away dust out of the air. Create images that motivate a flicking action. Flick with various body parts. Move about the space. Explore, discover, and observe. Integrate the body, mind, and spirit. Add sound and then words. Let the voice reflect the body movements.

Float is a combination of light weight, indirect space, and sustained time. Fill your torso with air and let it float. Let an arm float and wave. Float to the floor. Float and roll or recline as if you were floating like a cloud. Explore many ways to float. Add sound and words.

The eight basic actions have many derivations. Here are a few examples to use as a guide. When you work with an action for a selected scene and character what is its LMA action drive?

Punch: bang, bash, clobber, hit, slug, clap, thrust, stab, pound.

Press: rub, pierce, tear, grind, pull, knead, compress.

Slash: whip, rip, gash, knife, swat, cane, snatch, gore.

Wring: mash, wrench, gnaw, bind, massage, furrow, twist.

Dab: poke, bat, tug, pat, stick, knock, shake, snip.

Glide: comb, smooth, wipe, draw, scrape, stir, peel, smear.

Flick: jerk, fling, waft, strike, fan, ruffle, flip, nip, toss.

Float: arise, cradle, caress, suspend, stroke, nuzzle, unfold.

Exercise: Movement Score with Actions

1. Create a simple movement score with a clear objective and the use of two LMA action drives. Example of a simple movement score: Enter a room, cross to a table, pull out a chair, sit, sort through some papers, rearrange the papers into tidy stacks, stand, push the chair back to the table, exit. You might begin in a float action drive and after sitting move into a flick action drive. Use your imagination and creativity.

2. Review when the action change occurred and why. Repeat the movement score and clarify the movement choices based on objectives and action drives.

Exercise: Actions and Scene Study

1. Select a short scene that has more than three beats.

2. Select a scene objective.
3. Select an action for each beat from the eight basic actions. The choices and selections may come out of working through the scene. Find a balance between your intellectual perceptions through analysis and your interpretations that occur during rehearsal.

As you work through rehearsals you may discover some basic action derivatives are more suited for your interpretation. With each exploration, use the body fully. If your action is "to punch," then punch with all parts of the body. Later you can modify the physicality to appropriate behavior based on the given circumstances. Solidify your final action choices based on weight, time, and space values. Note: Action Drive is just one of the four drives Laban defined. Each Drive provides the actor many movement choices.

DYNAMICS AND INTENSITY

Dynamics refer to the variation of force during an action. A change within the action activates the dynamic shift. You might be working with the action "to punch" and it shifts to "bash" or "thrust." These are both derivatives of punch. Either change is a dynamic one. The use of dynamics gives movement patterns momentum and suspense. You may think of an action as being dynamic when a great degree of energy is used, but a dynamic change may mean a diminishing degree of energy as well as a vibrant alteration. The degree of energy used will be marked by the intensity level. Intensity is the amount of concentration, power, or force given to the movement.

Exercise: Dynamics and Intensity

1. Select a who, what, when, where, and why for an improvisation.
2. Choose an objective and action to begin the improvisation.
3. Physicalize the action with one body part at a time until the entire body is engaged.
4. Alter the dynamics by incorporating action derivatives.
5. Adjust the intensity of the movement by increasing or diminishing the action's power and concentration.
6. When appropriate or necessary change the action and explore how to use dynamics and intensity to move the dramatic action forward.

Enjoy the movement for its own value. Stay in the moment and be spontaneous. Invest in the connection between your physical and psychological experience and behavior.

SUMMARY

The three basic elements of movement (space, time, and weight) can be explored throughout your life. Your sense of space, time, and weight is constantly being altered as perceptions of yourself and the world are reevaluated. The discovery of these element's complexity and vitality can be enlightening during the acting process. Pursue an in-depth look at qualitative and quantitative values of space, time, and weight. Create actions and value what you find during the process. Use your discoveries in the future as a reference point.

JOURNAL ENTRIES

Describe your perceptions about space and spatial relationships.

Describe your action preferences. Describe how you used action drives in a movement score.

Describe a situation and circumstances you recently experienced with time values. Did you use a rest, an accent, or tempo changes? Was the time quality quick or sustained? How was physical behavior influenced?

Discuss your observations, impressions, additional exercises, and ideas for future reference.

ENVIRONMENT, PROPERTIES, AND COSTUMES

ENVIRONMENT: PERSON

Environment influences behavior and physicality. It stimulates emotions by creating feelings that range from freedom to claustrophobia, security to terror, warmth to freezing, and many other reactions. The significance of the relationship between the environment and psychological process is recognized by behavioral scientists. By exploring how environment influences behavior you will gain a greater understanding about your personal responses to different environmental factors and build a foundation for character choices.

Sensory perceptions of surroundings are a determining factor in physical and psychological responses. You may have personal reactions to specific environments that can be channeled into insights for use as an actor and ultimately to enhance character choices. Beginning with sight, consider everything you see. Are you indoors or outdoors? Are there trees, flowers, birds, grass, a stream, clouds, desert, mud, snow, buildings, or traffic? If you are indoors what is the shape of the room? Does it have a high or low ceiling? Is the room wide or narrow? What are the textures of the walls and floors? How many doors? What is on the walls? Are there pictures or photographs? What is the response to the environmental elements?

Just as your personal behavior is influenced by what you see, hear, taste, touch, and smell, a similar response can be discovered and interpreted for a character you are portraying. Review the details about the environment. What is the climate? Is it raining, snowing, windy? Is the place hot, cold, wet, dry? Is the environment cramped, open, soothing, unsettling? What is in your line of vision? Do you hear other people, animals, sounds of nature, machinery, sounds that are comforting, or sounds that concern you? Do you taste anything? What are your tactile sensations? What can you smell? How do these sensory observations affect your behavior?

Exercise: Climate as a Plant

Embodying a plant and experiencing changes in climate can give you a sense of freedom from predictable human behavior. Select a familiar plant for the movement study.

1. React to the following stimuli. You are a seedling buried in the earth, surrounded and supported by cool, moist soil. Drink in the nutrients from the soil. Begin to germinate, sprout, and grow. You are expanding with each breath. Feel yourself pushing through the earth as you grow, feel the sunrays pulling you up and out. Your roots drink in moisture as they coil deeper into the soil. You have reached full growth. It is warm, and the sun is pouring over your body. There is a gentle breeze, and the sunrays are becoming warmer. It becomes hot and dry. The wind has stopped. Clouds drift overhead. It is becoming cool and pleasant. It begins to rain softly. Respond to the water trickling down your stems, petals, branches, and leaves. The raindrops are coming down faster and heavier. You are in the midst of a hailstorm. Respond to the small hailstones slamming down. It is cold and wet and violent. The hail and rain is blown away and it is night. It is cool, and it begins to snow. Soft snowflakes settle on you. The snow begins to weigh you down and is surrounding your roots. The snow stops. Respond to the cold, wet heaviness of the packed snow. It is morning, and the sun is out and the snow is melting away. The climate becomes warm and pleasant again. Ideal conditions and environment surround you.

Discuss various physical and psychological responses to the stimuli. How were your breath, energy, heart rate, and senses affected as a result of changing climate images?

Exercise: Climate and Personal Response

1. Imagine a climate and list its elements. Is the sun out? Is it midday, early evening, or night? Is it hot, dry, wet, cold, humid, arid, windy, calm, etc.?
2. Select three qualities from the list (hot, dry, and windy, or calm, cold, and wet) and physicalize each one separately to create three short movement studies.
3. Connect the three studies to form one physical statement. Repeat the statement over and over, slowly transforming it into a final form.
4. Create a one-minute movement study based on your personal response to a specific climate.

How did the movement study reflect your physical and psychological behavior and the climate? What did you discover about your perception of this particular climate? In what ways can you relate this study to acting?

Exercise: Sensory Responses to Environment

1. Experience a selected environment and make a detailed list of sensory impressions and facts about the environment. Is it restrictive or expansive? Does it have a high ceiling? Narrow passages? Can you run freely in the space? What is in your field of vision? What can you smell, touch, and hear? What other sensory responses do you have in the environment? Be specific.
2. Physicalize your response to three distinct sensory perceptions through sound and movement. Allow the motions to be bold and visual.
3. String your sound and movement responses together to create a physical statement. How do these motions convey the environment's essence?
4. Keep repeating the abstract sound and movement and slowly let the movement become realistic.
5. Create a one-minute realistic movement study clarifying your relationship to the environment based on sensory responses.

ENVIRONMENT: ACTOR

The following exercises are designed to be shared in the classroom. You are using your heightened sense of awareness to communicate a believable specific environment.

Exercise: Relationship to Environment

1. Physicalize an environment you have experienced through detailed activity. Involve all your senses.
2. Focus on your relationship to the environment. Why are you there? Are the surroundings familiar? Are you alone? If someone else is there, what is your relationship? How does another person, or being alone, affect your relationship to this environment?
3. Share your environment study with others. How can you show where you are without language and without indicating the environment with stereotypical behavior?

What physical behavior was used to suggest the environment? How were breath, alignment, gesture, weight, time, and space used?

Exercise: Relationship to Others in Environment

1. Begin a simple activity within a specific environment. Make it clear where you are and what you are doing. You may use sound but not dialogue.
2. One at a time the observers will join you in the environment and activity. Respond to the new person. How does the environment change? After physically interacting, dialogue may be used but not to describe the action or place.

What sensory aspects were you able to physicalize? What environmental conditions are more readily accessible? If you observed the activity, describe the physical behavior and what it communicated about the environment.

PROPERTIES

How an actor uses a property (prop) may define character and dramatic action. The character's motivation, intention, and subtext may be seen through the way the actor handles a prop. It becomes an extension of the character and illustrates emotions and desires.

Properties may be categorized as hand props, set props, and costume props. Hand props are objects that can be picked up and manipulated. Examples of hand props are a book, glass, or feather duster. A set prop is a permanent object within the setting that defines the environment or scenic concept. Examples of set props might include furniture, like a chair or lamp, or a large item like a wagon. A costume prop is an accessory that is part of the dress. Examples of costume props include an apron, tie, or hat.

Properties may be used functionally. A fan is used to cool oneself, a glass to sip a drink from, a newspaper to read. Or, they may be used expressively to illustrate character objectives and emotions. A fan may be used to seduce someone or a book may be hurled across the room in a fit of anger. Whether functional or expressive, the prop should be used to highlight the action and/or character. A prop should not be used arbitrarily and become a distraction in the action or characterization.

Study the property before exploration. Look at it and feel its texture, shape, and weight. What is its intended function? How can it be held, carried, and moved? How many different uses can you find for it? Can it be transformed to represent other objects?

If the property has a functional use and is expected to be utilized in a truthful manner then it is the actor's responsibility to understand its conventional usage. If it is a weapon the actor must know how the weapon is carried, how it is held and used in attack or defense. If it is a hand prop like a cigarette and the actor has never smoked, but is required to do so for the role, the actor must learn how to smoke in a truthful manner. If the character is seen writing a letter the actor must write something instead of scribbling a few lines. If the audience is to believe that the character is reading a book and absorbing information then the actor must see the words rather than glance at the page. The action must be preplanned and rehearsed so that it is truthful and not an obstacle during performance.

Exercise: Functional Use of Properties

1. Select a prop. Feel its shape, texture, and weight. See its form and color. Physically respond to what you see and feel.
2. Hold it, carry it, toss it, and move it about at various tempos. Move it up, down, and as many ways as you can imagine.
3. Use the prop functionally. If it is a book, read it; if it is a chair, sit on it; if it is a drink, quench your thirst. Discover ways of using the prop as it was intended.

Exercise: Expressive Use of Properties

1. Select a prop. Study its form, texture, weight, and all other aspects using sensory perceptions.
2. Discover expressive behaviors using the prop. Go beyond the property's conventional usage. Examples: A scarf could be used to grab someone; a pencil may be used to pry open a drawer; a cane can be used to pick up trash, etc.

How is the property an extension of your emotions, point of view, or desire? How do you communicate with the property? Record your perceptions in your journal.

Exercise: Personalization of Properties

1. Select a prop from your home.
2. What does the prop mean to you? What is its value and significance? How long have you had it? Why do you use it? What is its history?
3. Share the importance and background about your prop with another person.
4. Use the prop both functionally and as an expression of your inner life.

Did your perception of the property and how you used it change after you shared its importance and background with another?

Exercise: Use of Set Properties

1. Start with a chair to study the use of a set property. Discover different ways of sitting on the chair. After adjusting into each position, acknowledge how the position affects your self-image or the image you project.
2. Create different stationary positions around the chair while sustaining contact.
3. Move on or around the chair. Move about the chair while having intermittent contact.
4. Move the chair to another location. Work with rhythms, tempos, and energies.

Experience the same exercise using other set props, such as a bench, tree stump, sofa, and other pieces that might be permanent parts of a set.

Exercise: Basic Actions and Properties

1. Select a prop. Discover sensory perceptions about the property. Consider how it feels, looks, smells, sounds, and tastes.
2. Explore movement possibilities using float, punch, glide, dab, slash, flick, wring, and press actions. Keep yourself open to physical and psychological responses.
3. Use the property both functionally and expressively.

COSTUMES

The costume you wear will most likely dictate how you move more so than any other external element within a production. The weight, form, style, texture, and structure will govern how your body moves. For instance, if it is a heavy period garment it will demand specific physical adjustments. The costume may fit tightly around the shoulders or waist. You will need to assess your movement potential and the character's needs. It is not only the restrictions that you must review but also how the costume defines the character.

Clothing is very personal, and communicates who you are. Before the twentieth century most clothing was built from scratch. The fabric, cut, style, and accessories were hand-selected. Contemporary clothing is still sometimes built for individuals by hand, but much more often clothing is bought from the rack in retail stores. In either circumstance personal clothing choices and creating a desired public image typically is given careful consideration. You can analyze a character's costume choices for information about the character, as well as seeing how the costume's structure influences behavior.

Just as a costume helps define the character's identity, so does your attire project a personal image. To better understand how costumes can assist you as an actor first acknowledge your own fashion preferences.

Exercise: Personal Fashion Preferences

1. Look at yourself in a full-length mirror. Describe what you see. What image do you project? Do not be judgmental, but rather be descriptive and objective.
2. Examine what you chose to wear. Why did you select these clothes? Was it a conscious decision

made with forethought, or was it a haphazard choice? Was the selection made by the activities you had planned today, or by a need to make a fashion statement?
3. Look closely at what you are wearing and find the breaking points in the dress. The breaking points are those areas that allow movement of the major joints like the shoulder, elbow, wrist, neck, waist, hips, and ankles. How much mobility do the garments and accessories allow?
4. Stand, walk, sit, lie down, tip toe, skip, jump, gallop, run fast and slow, fall, roll, move all about. Move through as many different levels, directions, and ranges of motion that your clothing will facilitate.

What clothes do you like to wear for leisure? What type do you wear for your job, for a social occasion, or for work around the yard or house? What colors and types of fabrics do you like to wear? What types of shoes and accessories do you wear? How does your dress affect your physical, social, and psychological behavior? Observe and describe others physicalizations and projected images.

SHOES

Shoes may be the primary costume element that dictates physical carriage. They are important because they influence your alignment and placement, and thereby affect your breath and energy. The higher and more narrow the heel, the more your placement will shift forward. The spine will make adjustments so the body will balance and remain upright. If the sole is soft there will be more articulation of the numerous joints in the foot, allowing you to move fast and be more nimble. You will be more likely to run, jump, skip, and exercise greater locomotor skills if the shoes are flexible and comfortable.

Exercise: Shoes

1. Select three contrasting pairs of shoes. One pair might be a type of sport shoe, another a formal shoe, and another a work shoe.
2. Stand barefooted. Articulate the joints. Feel the floor underneath. Feel the weight placement. How does standing on bare feet affect your

alignment? Walk, run, skip, and jump. Work with varying tempos and manner of movement.

3. Put on a pair of shoes. Stand and acknowledge how they make you feel. How do they alter your placement and alignment?

4. Begin walking. Walk slowly at first, then build up speed. How is walking in shoes different from being barefooted? How has your physicality been affected? How do the shoes make you feel?

5. Explore different ways of moving by finding various levels, ranges of motion, and directions. Do the shoes affect energy?

How did the shoes adjust your physicality? What emotional and behavioral responses surfaced?

GARMENTS

Garments are any article of clothing worn on the torso, pelvis, legs, and arms. They are the main body of your wardrobe and are not considered accessories, which should be examined separately. Garments allow or restrict motion directly affecting behavior. They also project a public image through silhouette and style.

Exercise: Garments and Physical Behavior

1. Select a garment. It may be a shirt, jacket, trousers or robe, etc., but not an accessory such as a hat, scarf, or gloves.

2. Before putting the garment on examine how it is constructed. How is it built? Where are the seams? What is the cut and style? What is the texture of the fabric? What is the weight?

3. Put the garment on and look at your silhouette in a full-length mirror. What image do you project? How does the garment drape or hang? What does it feel like in terms of tightness, heaviness, comfort, and fabric texture against the body? When you move does the garment flow or is it rigid?

4. Move about the space. Work with various levels, directions, ranges of motion, actions, tempos, stationary and locomotor activities.

5. What is your emotional and psychological response to wearing the garment?

SUMMARY

The study of environment, properties, and costumes is a very practical approach to understanding more about yourself and acting choices. Every day you respond to the environment and objects that can be used functionally and expressively, and each day you use clothing to define yourself. These elements can be extensions of the self and actor in preparation for characterization. Discover how you can improve your physical communication through their use.

JOURNAL ENTRIES

Describe a way the environment influences your behavior.

Describe a psychological and physical response to a specific climate.

Describe a use of a garment to suggest character, desire, or conflict. This can be through self-observation or that of another person.

Process your observations, impressions, additional exercises, and ideas for future reference.

How do shoes affect your physicality and point of view? Review a specific situation and/or event when your shoes affected your behavior.

Part Three

Character

Connecting the person to actor to character is a challenging artistic quest. Part Two defined the person and actor aspects of the trinity. You are ready to complete the triad by adding the vision of a character.

In Part Three the person, actor, and character are unified. Many of the same exercises you worked through to define person and actor are modified to create character movement choices. You will make characterization choices based upon inspiration, observation, discovery, and interpretation through creative projects. The personal and acting resources enhanced in Part Two are streamlined into characterization.

The terms objective, obstacle, action, and given circumstances will be used for the creative projects. An objective is what the character wants, needs, or desires. When playing a character, ask yourself, "What do I want?" It can be an overall objective for the action of the play, a scene objective, or a moment-to-moment objective. An obstacle is the conflict presented, preventing an easy attainment of the objective. It can be another person, a concept, or a situation. Ask "What is preventing me from getting what I want?" The action is how the character actively pursues the objective with the obstacle in focus. To analyze the action, ask "What am I willing to do to get what I want?" Given circumstances are factual elements influencing charac-

ter, story, and plot. This will include but is not limited to: time of day, previous action, environment, climate, as well as social, economic, political, moral, and religious circumstances. Specific given circumstances for a character include but are not limited to: age, health, and occupation. Analyze the script carefully for the given circumstances.

Selected characters are presented in the "Case Studies" section for reference, thought, and discussion. The characters are taken from a wide range of periods to provide a broad base of application of movement studies. Any case study may be used as a study method or model for another character.

You might choose to study one character for all the creative projects in Part Three. This gives you a process of characterization with great depth. Or, you might work on various characters for a broader range of experiences.

The study of concepts and exercises in parts One and Two can be enriching as you expand your movement potential and make observations and discoveries about your personal and acting preferences. The applications to character in Part Three can be rewarding. This is when you have the opportunity to channel your creative choices into an acting process. It is your process and your choices that are implemented to create a unique character interpretation.

CHARACTER AND RELAXATION

You are now ready to begin the journey of building a characterization by applying previously studied exercises to your acting process. If you fully explored relaxation as a person and actor, the sensations and movements will fall into place with ease. Your body has a kinesthetic sense of remembering past experiences. Begin with the relaxation process. While relaxation is your focus, incorporate elements of alignment, center, space, time, and weight. Stay in tune with your physical and psychological responses as you link movement to acting choices.

PROJECT: CHARACTER STUDY USING THE SEVEN STATES OF BEING

Select a character and monologue. Answer basic acting questions: What is my objective? What is my obstacle? What is my action? Refer to the "Case Studies" section and the case study of Laura Wingfield from *The Glass Menagerie* for an example of a detailed analysis.

1. Start in comfortable position. Use a relaxation exercise to focus and center. Release and let go of tension that will block creativity.
2. Drop in the breath as you let the body begin to take the character's physical shape and alignment. Start from the feet and work up through the skeletal frame to the head. Ask and answer questions at a semi-audible level about your objective, obstacle, action, age, health, disposition, and occupation. With each answer allow your body to redefine its shape, breath, and center as needed. Focus on "What is my objective?" Let the answer feed the general disposition and overall tension level.
3. Use the Seven States of Being exercise in Part Two as a means to compare tension levels and

explore moment to moment. For example, you might begin with the Leisure state of being and then the intensity increases and you transform into the Pipe Cleaner start and finish in Dramatic Action. The important part of the process is to be able to physicalize varying degrees of relaxation and tension and mold with dynamics. Don't try to make something happen. Let yourself experience moment to moment.
4. Create a movement study without words. It can be approximately the same length of time as the monologue, but ultimately it depends on your needs as an actor.

Let yourself experience the varying states of the character's relaxation and tension. Indulge yourself with time for experiences and discoveries. The monologue may be only two to four minutes, but you need adequate time to explore the character's objective, obstacle, and actions, and let those filter into the relaxation and tension levels needed to create a credible character. Give yourself permission to investigate the character solely for differing levels of relaxation and tension.

5. Share the movement study with others. What was communicated? Observers need to describe what they saw, and not what they would have liked to have seen or what they expected. The observer should try to be specific about the physical choices made by the actor. Listen to the observations and note changes you might like to incorporate. Focus on relaxation and tension levels and their use in defining character choices.

After working through the piece without words and focusing on relaxation you are more able to make character choices that have depth and clarity.

You are able to define your art based on inspiration and interpretation.

6. Repeat the movement study and add the dialogue. Transform the movement study as needed to discover an exciting presentation.

SUMMARY

Begin the process of applying relaxation to character interpretation by first addressing your personal and actor relaxation needs. Acknowledge your physical tension and release by using a relaxation technique. Once you have entered into a state of balance and are relaxed you are more able to begin the characterization process. Be specific with relaxation and tension character choices. Anchor your choices in the information given by the playwright.

JOURNAL ENTRIES

What connections did you make between relaxation/tension states and characterization?

What relaxation/tension choices did you make for a monologue and character, and why?

Process additional observations, impressions, and ideas for future reference.

What did you learn that you can use in a rehearsal process?

CHARACTER AND ALIGNMENT

Once you have acknowledged your personal alignment and can easily shift to a neutral alignment you are ready to create a character's alignment. Many times your physical shape illustrates more of who you are than what you say. Your physical behavior is a major part of your identity. You can often identify people from long distances by their alignment, walking patterns, and overall physical behavior. As your physical shape identifies your personality in daily life so too can a character's physical shape identify personality, needs, and conflict for an audience.

Review your physical, emotional, and vocal mannerisms, and look for behavioral patterns. You should be able to define your personality and link it to your physical preferences. For instance, you may define yourself as assertive and goal-oriented. This may be linked to the reason you walk with heavy steps and your placement is forward, causing you to appear to be in a hurry to get somewhere. Or you may feel out of touch with your present environment and ill at ease around strangers. This may adjust your alignment to where the upper body is curved forward while the hips are tucked under and one knee is relaxed. Before developing a character's alignment complete a thorough character analysis. Be able to readily verbalize the character's physical, mental, vocal, and psychological traits just as you would your own.

Identify the character's unique qualities and distinguish similar and contrasting behavior in yourself, both verbally and physically. Keep going back to information given by the playwright, or through reviews and interviews. Use whatever sources are available. The best information source is the script, where dialogue and physical actions provide facts.

PROJECT: ALIGNMENT CHANGES WITHIN A MONOLOGUE

Refer to the case study of Rosalind from *As You Like It* for an analysis connecting alignment and characterization.

1. Select a character and monologue. In a neutral stance, focus on the character's objective, obstacle, and action. As the character, talk through the answers. Let the alignment be informed as you speak. Talk through given circumstances such as age, health, and occupation or any contributing fact that would shape the body.
2. Work through the monologue without words. Focus on the alignment and changes. Be sensitive to changes in thought, desire, conflict, and expectations. When a change occurs does the body adjust the alignment? When could an alteration in the alignment communicate an internal change? The adjustment can be subtle and still inform you and an audience about the character.
3. Create a movement study focusing on alignment. Work without words.
4. Add the text.

For this exercise it is best to use a monologue that fluctuates in thought and mood. However, any monologue in which the character grows will serve as well. As you work through the monologue and reshape your alignment check for unnecessary collapses in the spine, especially the head and neck. A teacher can guide you through a means of working with a character alignment while minimizing physical misuse.

PROJECT: CHARACTERIZATION AND ALIGNMENT

Select a character and scene for study. Choose objectives, obstacles, actions, and given circumstances. Select three primary character traits, which are aspects and qualities that define personality.

1. Start in neutral and concentrate on one of the character traits. Let it shape your body from the feet up to the head. How does the character trait affect the position of the feet? Are the knees bent? Are the hips thrust forward, back, to the side, or dropped in the center? Are the abdominal muscles pulled in and up or dropped? How are the ribs positioned? Are the shoulders pushed back, rounded forward, hunched up, uneven, or relaxed? Do the arms hang limply, or are the elbows bent and the hands clasped? Is the neck long, or the jaw jutted forward? Does the head tilt forward, side, back, or is it held erect? There are numerous possibilities.
2. Go through the same process concentrating on another trait, and then the third.
3. Let the three traits mix and shape the alignment.
4. Use a mirror and be perceptive about what you see.
5. Share your alignment movement study with others. Listen to the description of the alignment you have created. Do not explain or defend your choices. Listen and evaluate your choices based on the description. Adjust your interpretation if needed.

Variations on this project may address social, economic, and environmental circumstances. You might also go through the same process and concentrate on objectives, obstacles, action, and beat changes. When working with beat changes experience if and how the character's alignment adjusts to the new focus or direction of the action. In each process begin in neutral and then focus on a specific given circumstance that will impact the alignment.

SUMMARY

Character alignment is central to readily identifying a personality. The shape, form, and silhouette have immediate impact upon the viewer. More importantly, adjustments in alignment have significant relevance for your psychological outlook. If you are open to new insights about yourself you will unlock a powerhouse of body-mind-spirit connections and channel the experiences into your acting through alignment adjustments.

JOURNAL ENTRIES

What did you discover about the relationship between alignment and characterization that you could use in a rehearsal process?

Outline specific alignment choices and adjustments for character and scene.

Process additional observations, impressions, and ideas for future reference.

CHARACTER AND BREATH

A primary factor concerning breath and character is that your breath is connected to impulses and informs behavior. To achieve this you will need to access a full and responsive breath pattern before beginning an exploration. The breath pattern can and will likely change based on the character's circumstances and actions. This will happen when you are in the moment, centered, and intellectually and emotionally available.

Use breathing explorations to gain insight about the interpretation of a specific moment, action, and emotion. Breath can release emotional and physical blocks, which may prevent full communication.

Two case studies are outlined as reference material and models for the following projects. They are taken from *The Glass Menagerie* and *Arms and the Man*.

PROJECT: EXPLORING A SCENE WITH BREATH

Select a character and scene for exploration. Analyze the script and scene for the objective, obstacle, and actions. Do not discuss your analysis with your partner until after the first exploration. This will support more opportunities for surprise and spontaneity.

1. Start in neutral. Speak at a semi-audible level as the character. Talk about who you are, where you are, what the situation is, your objective, obstacle, and actions. Talk about anything that seems important. As you are talking you are in motion. Let the breath and body respond.
2. Experience an emotional quality flowing out of the movement. Let your breathing patterns express your thoughts and feelings. Do not use words. Communicate the scene's essence with breath, then add nonverbal sounds.

3. Work by yourself, then work with a scene partner. Interact character to character using only breath, then nonverbal sounds and breath, and finally add dialogue.

Review the communication of ideas in the scene, and be objective about moments needing specific attention. Repeat portions or the entire process as needed.

PROJECT: CHARACTER AND BREATH

Refer to the case studies for an analysis of the first scene in George Bernard Shaw's *Arms and the Man* and as a possible source of study.

1. Select and analyze a scene with a partner. Record the given circumstances and discuss. What is your character's objective, obstacle, and action? Keep this information to yourself during the first exploration.
2. Stand in neutral and close your eyes. Let the breath be free to drop in and release. Focus on how you feel and the space you occupy. Let yourself become centered.
3. With each breath draw in the character's life-force bit by bit. Feel the character's alignment, placement, weight, and center evolving. Connect to the character's breath pattern at the scene's beginning.
4. Focus on your immediate objective. Say it over and over to yourself semi-audibly. If you are working from the *Arms and the Man* scene you have either just entered a stranger's room at night as you are trying to escape from being killed, or you are hiding under the blankets and see a man enter your room. Both Bluntschli and Raina are in need of escaping danger. What is their objective, obstacle, and action?

5. Let the breathing pattern be shaped by the character's objective.

6. Open the eyes and move from the stationary position through space. Physicalize letting breath be the movement impulse. Work with a nonliteral interpretation of behavior. Explore the space, time, and weight factors. Keep returning to the objective, obstacle, action, and the expectation of getting what you want.

7. Slowly transform the abstract movement to conventional behavior. Work through the character's physical activity.

8. Release nonverbal sounds such as sighs, laughter, cries, grunts, or any other sounds that are organic to the moment and action.

9. Find your partner while maintaining the exploration and begin the scene. Accent the use of breath on impulse. Let the breath heighten your awareness and emotions.

What connections were made between your objective and breath? What changes in the breath occurred as you transformed into the character? Why? What movements evolved as you abstractly explored the objective? Was the breath connected to the movement? What did you discover about yourself and the character? How did you react to the other? Did the breath change? Did the movement change? Why? How? Keep asking yourself questions so that you can create a solid connection among breath, action, and character.

SUMMARY

Continually be aware of connecting breath with motion and emotion during the working process. Breath responds to impulses and informs behavior. When breath is not connected to activity and action then the creative process and product are diminished. In addition, use breath as a tool for digging into the character's body, mind, and spirit. The changes in breath can be subtle and must always be organic. Keep referring to the objectives and moment-to-moment changes in the scene.

JOURNAL ENTRIES

What connections did you make between breath and character? What specific changes did you explore?

Process additional observations, impressions, and ideas for future reference.

CHARACTER AND CENTER

The discovery of a character's center may be approached by analyzing and exploring the character's internal life and external physical conditions. An analysis of the internal life considers the character's objectives, obstacles, and actions. External factors determining the character's center are based on given circumstances. Both the internal and external circumstances contribute to physical and psychological characteristics. Any factor influencing behavior should be considered.

After making a detailed character analysis, make a list of similarities and dissimilarities between yourself and the character. When this is done and you feel secure in sensing your personal and preferred actor center, connect to an ideal center and feel balanced, focused, and present, then establish the character's center.

A psychological center may be selected based on the character's internal life. The emotional and behavioral characteristics are the guideposts for interpreting a psychological center. Review the character's mental processes and determine whether the character's needs seem to originate from the spiritual (heart), power (solar plexus), or survival (abdomen).

PROJECT: CHARACTER CENTER AND CHOICE

Select and analyze a character and monologue. Explore the monologue using the three centers: heart, solar plexus, and abdomen. You can adapt this exercise to other potential centers that you might find more appropriate.

Refer to the *Summer and Smoke* case study as a possible source and model for this project.

1. Bring the character to life using alignment, placement, energy, relaxation/tension, and other resources you find beneficial.
2. Focus on the heart center. Breathe into the center. Color the breath. Give it substance. Feel the chest expand and release. Physically stimulate the chest with touch: pat, stroke, massage. Activate the center with sound, using "ay" as in play. Move with the sound. Allow the character to transform rather than trying to hold on to a preconceived ideal form and behavior. Connect to the spiritual or romantic character qualities as you say "I love" and continue movement. When ready, speak as the character using sentences beginning with "I love." Let the chest originate the movement. After full exploration speak as the character using text with the chest as center.
3. Stay with the character's essence, but shift your focus and awareness to the solar plexus center. Breath into the center. Use imagery with the breath. Physically activate the center with touch or with large movements like contractions. Let sound touch the center with vibrations using the vowel sound "ah" as in father. Connect with the need for power as you say "I can" from the center. Move through space allowing transformation of the character with the solar plexus center. When ready, complete phrases beginning with "I can." Let the solar plexus center initiate movement. Begin using the text. Explore the monologue and character using the solar plexus as center.
4. Maintain the character's essence and shift your focus to the abdomen center. Breathe into the center. Use imagery if helpful. Physically activate the center with breath, touch, or with large movements such as circling the pelvis. Let sound radiate from the center using the vowel sound "oo" as in due. Connect with the need for survival as you say "I want," and; when ready, complete sentences or phrases beginning with "I want." Let the abdomen center initiate movement. Let the character transform. Explore the monologue with this center.

What did you experience and discover about the character from each center? Are there aspects of each center in the character? Which center works best for the character and for you? Why? If you feel another center like the head might better serve the character, use the same process.

Michael Chekhov in *To the Actor* illustrates the point of exploring various centers and the impulse you might experience: "If you were to move the center from your chest to your head, you would become aware that the thought element has begun to play a characteristic part in your performance." He goes on to suggest that "if you put a soft, warm, not too small center in the region of your abdomen you may experience a psychology that is self-satisfied, earthy, a bit heavy and even humorous." Be sensitive to these possibilities and make choices that enable you to create a finely defined character that responds moment to moment.

SUMMARY

Once you grasp the concept of center you can begin to differentiate between the origins of your movement and those of the characters you are creating. By identifying the character's center you can distinguish the area that initiates the character's movement and thus enrich the portrayal. When you are centered as the character you will sense power, unity, focus, and balance. You will find the resources from within to follow impulses and create spontaneity. Discover the process that works best for you.

JOURNAL ENTRIES

Describe your choice of center and the physical adjustments based on a character exploration.

Process additional observations, impressions, and ideas for future reference

CHARACTER: SOUND AND MOVEMENT

In Part One, sound and movement for the person and actor touched upon the basic union between vibration and physicalization. You are now ready to let sound come forward through the character's spirit, and respond to its depth and richness. Sound pulsates through the body and generates movement. It is a force that flows through the body. It can sculpt your physicality through the use of breath, tone, pitch, volume, vibration, and when combining various sounds to form words.

In the following project you will blend sound and responses from a character's needs, wants, and emotions. You will then connect sound to the formation of words, phrases, and script. As the intellectual demands of the text become more sophisticated, let yourself return to the basic premise of sound vibrations creating movement responses. Let sound reflect primal instincts.

PROJECT: SOUND AND MOVEMENT WITH A MONOLOGUE

Select a character and monologue for all four parts of this project.

Part One: Emotion

1. Physicalize the character focusing on alignment, breath, and center.
2. What is the character's objective and obstacle? Let your physical shape transform. What emotion is expressed? The emotion will be a by-product expressed out of the objective and obstacle demands. Explore a simple sound and movement that express the emotion's essence.
3. Work through the monologue using the sound and movement. Does the emotional base change from the beginning to end? If so, discover a simple sound and movement phrase for the emotional essence of the monologue's beginning, middle, and end. The sound and movement phrases should be economical, precise, and fully engage the character's body, mind, and spirit.
4. Connect the sound and movement phrases together in a physical statement that embodies the emotional changes. Keep repeating the statement until the sounds and movements have clarity and precision.
5. Use the sound and movement statement as you work through the character's action and monologue. Be true to the sound and movement quality and impression.

How does the physical expression affect the vocal expression? How does the sound and movement statement shape the intensity of the character's objective? What did you discover about the emotional attitude?

Part Two: Vowel and Consonant Sounds

1. Vocalize a single vowel or consonant sound the character uses and release with movement. The sound will start from the center and radiate through the body. Let the breath and sound be one. Explore the sound and movement and find many qualities. Sense the sound's shape affecting the body's shape. The sound and movement need to be impulsive; don't force the response. Connect the need to communicate with the physicalization and vocalization.
2. Work through the monologue and process the physicalization through the vowel and consonant sound exploration.

How do the sound and movement complement

or contrast one another? How does the vowel sound "o" differ in sound and movement from "e?" How does the consonant sound of "d" differ in movement and sound from "n?" How did the key vowel sounds influence the character's physical behavior?

Part Three: Syllables and Movement

1. Vocalize a syllable the character uses and release movement. Explore many ways of expressing the syllable with movement. Experience the full shape of the sound through the body. Give over to the sound coming from within and being physicalized involuntarily.
2. Connect two or more syllables and movements together without forming any words. The sound and movement flow together like phrases composing a character statement.
3. Work through the monologue using sound and movement syllable discoveries.

Part Four: Syllables to Words and Movement

1. Explore the sound and movement possibilities of syllables that may be formed into words. Examples: she-nan-i-gan, ir-ri-tate, and fan-ta-sy to form the words shenanigan, irritate, and fantasy. Physicalize each syllable and connect to others to form the word with a sound and movement phrase. Find the word's meaning in its sounds and physicalization.
2. Select several key words that the character speaks. Physicalize the syllables and connect to form words. Connect the physicalization and word sounds to the character's action.

Use the process of this project to explore the meaning and interpretation of poetry, songs, monologues, and scenes. Break the words down to the most basic sounds and fully explore the physical range of motion. You may find deeper interpretations.

Project: Tossing Sound, Text, and Movement with Others

1. Pair up with a scene partner.
2. One person tosses a sound and movement. The receiver tosses back a responding sound and movement. Continue this until you feel that the responses are flowing easily and spontaneously from person to person.
3. Begin tossing words and movement to each other. Continue this until the responses are exchanged without intellectually monitored impulses. Trust your instinct.
4. Physically transform into the character. Sound and shape phrases and sentences. Allow the dialogue to flow back and forth from character to character. Impulsively respond to each other's sound and movement.

As dialogue is added to the work invest in the character's physical presence. Explore the character's physicality through sound in relation to word choice. Keep the physicalization bold. Trust the unity of body, mind, and spirit to work in harmony.

SUMMARY

Sound can add fullness to a character's physical life. When sound flows through the body it adds color to the movement. It is a primal expression of need and expectation. It generates energy and intensifies actions. It must come from the spirit, be generated through the body, and shaped with the mind.

JOURNAL ENTRIES

How does movement influence sound? How did you connect a sound exploration to a selected character study?

In what way did the creation and play with sound and movement phrases create new insights about a characterization?

Process examples of how movements were generated by syllables.

Process additional observations, impressions, and ideas for future reference.

CHARACTER AND IMAGERY

Linking imagery studies to the process of developing a character's physical life can greatly expand your acting choices. When the imagination is open and you allow yourself to take risks new movement choices previously dormant may be actualized. The power of the mind to shape and influence the body is remarkable.

The process of using image studies is based on the corresponding work in Part Two. Begin with an animal study. The process will be the same as previously explored, but now linked to a scripted character.

PROJECT: ANIMAL IMAGERY AND CHARACTERIZATION

Select an animal that shares a quality with a character you are rehearsing. Explore the animal behavior and mannerisms fully before transforming to the literal character behavior. Take your time.

1. Settle into a comfortable position. Visualize the animal. See it in its natural habitat. Breathe in the animal's heartbeat. Adopt its spatial awareness, shape, focus, time, and weight.
2. Move and sound as the animal. Eat, rest, hunt, and play.
3. Transform into the character while maintaining the animal's sound and movement essence. Transform the animal's sound into human sounds. See the world as the character but maintain the animal's essential movement qualities. Choose not to speak but use sound on impulse.
4. Work through the physical activities while maintaining the animal's primal characteristics.
5. Add the dialogue. Allow the voice to be influenced by the animal's physical qualities.

What animal did you select for the character and why? What movement qualities did you discover about the character through the animal's behavior? How did you transfer the animal's physicalization to the character's? How was the physicalization affected when dialogue was utilized? Use your journal to record impressions.

PROJECT: ELEMENTS OF NATURE AND CHARACTER IMPROVISATION

1. Select an element of nature to embody—fire, earth, air, or water. Visualize and call out the element's qualities while moving. Bring the qualities to life.
2. Embody the element and focus on the qualities. Use sound, movement, and the entire space. Go from stationary to locomotor movement. Engage the body, mind, and spirit. Be spontaneous. Free your imagination. Be immediate, and avoid judgment of self or others.
3. Slowly modify the movement and sound to everyday behavior. Find how to walk, stand, sit, and gesture while embodying the element's essence.
4. Create a character out of the sound and movement patterns. Build a world for this character. When ready, speak and interact with others.

What type of character emerged from the essence of the element? Did you give over your entire self to the process? How did you interact with others? What happens when a personality dominated by the element of fire meets someone who is governed by water? What happens when fire meets air? Or when earth and water interact? What were you like when alone? What qualities of the element were most predominant in the character? What temperament emerged?

PROJECT: ESSENCE OF NATURE AND CHARACTER

Part One:

Utilize the element essence exercise for a scripted character. This is particularly helpful if you are having difficulty with a specific scene or action during rehearsal. You might find the energy, dynamics, and intensity the scene requires by selecting an element similar to a character's essence and then moving from abstract to conventional behavior while working through the scene. Because the element work totally engulfs the body it can help the actor to connect to the moment.

Part Two:

Use a season image for the character. Select a season that best represents the character's inner life. Embody the season. Let sound and movement release in the abstract and then transform into behavior. Let the season radiate through the character. Acknowledge any new character discoveries.

PROJECT: EVENT, OBJECT, COLOR, AND CHARACTER

Refer to the case studies for a brief outline of a scene in Williams's *The Glass Menagerie* as a possible source and/or model for study.

Part One: Event

1. Select a character and scene. Analyze the scene for the objective, obstacle, action, and given circumstances.
2. Center yourself as the character. You have a range of experiences to choose from to become the character. Know what works for you and use it—breath, alignment, placement, centering, space, time, etc.
3. What is your character experiencing? Engaging all of your senses, replay the event moment by moment in your mind. Let your breath, alignment, and energy respond to the images stirred by the recollection. Recall an event from your personal experience that evoked a similar response. Take your time so that your entire being experiences the event.

4. Find the event's essence and form a movement phrase using sound. Begin with the breath and let it be the movement impulse. Experience the connection of movement and images as you focus on the past event. You will begin with abstract movement patterns that will transform into an identifiable rhythm for the character. Create a sound and movement statement.
5. Keep repeating the sound and movement statement and add dialogue. Move to the scene with the movement phrase and dialogue and repeat it over and over as you slowly transform the movement phrase into conventional physical behavior.

Part Two: Essence and Object

1. Concentrate on the image of an object whose qualities are similar to the characterization you are exploring. What does it represent? Why? What meaning does it hold at this moment? Keep asking questions and let the answers shape your physicality. Be free to explore all sound and movement patterns that spring from the character's center.
2. Transform the sound and movement into an essence statement that represents a crucial moment. What is the character experiencing? What do you want? How do you express need, conflict, and expectation?
3. Repeat the essence statement until it is clear and focused.
4. Pair up with an actor playing the other character and repeat the movement phrase as you begin the action. Play through the scene with dialogue using the physicality of the movement statement suggested by the object's essence.

What did the essence study suggest about the scene and the character's physical nature? Discuss the alignment, breath connection, center, use of space, gestures, and movement patterns that emerged.

Part Three: Color and Character

1. Select a color that you feel best embodies the character's personality. Breathe the color into all parts of your body. Let the color radiate through your pores.

2. Connect sound, movement, and breath in response to the color. This creative activity will incorporate vocal and physical gestures that are abstractions of the color image with little or no identifiable references to everyday movement behavioral patterns.

3. Slowly transform the abstract movement into conventional behavior while the intensity and energy remains focused on the color image. The transformation must be slow to experience the richness of the abstraction filtering into conventional behaviors that are associated with daily activity.

4. Begin speaking as the character, letting the tone, texture, and range be influenced by the sound you unleashed while exploring the color image and the physical shapes created.

5. Work through a scene. Share with others.

What did you discover through the use of a color image? Was your breathing, alignment, placement, energy, focus, or vocal gesture changed because of the color image? Not all changes are large. Some of the more subtle physical choices have more meaning and depth in your growth as the character. Be open to all changes.

PROJECT: MUSIC AND CHARACTER IMPROVISATION

Exploring various elements of music—tempo, accent, rhythm, rests, crescendos, range of notes, etc.—can help you understand the similar values within a play and character.

1. Listen to a selection of music and let your body move.

2. Focus on the tempo and embody its momentum.

3. Stop the music, but keep the music's essence flowing through your body.

4. Create a character through the impulses generated by the music and movement response. Let a specific situation and activity take shape.

5. Maintain the character and activity, and play the music again. Focus on the music's tempo and the character's activity.

How did the music influence the behavior? What characteristics were brought forward? What was your behavior and action? How were your movements influenced by the tempo of the music?

Repeat the same process while focusing on the accents (stressed movements or sounds) within the music. Both music and drama have varying accents to highlight the composition. The actor uses accents to keep the character alive and dynamic.

Music and nonmusical sounds have a daily emotional impact on behavior and should be noted for use in the acting process. Be aware of your reactions to sounds and how they affect your physicality. Be open to new sensations and discoveries that sound stimulates. Connect those sensations to characterizations, emotions, and needs that acting challenges present.

SUMMARY

The power of images and essences can expand character choices beyond the realm of conventional behavior. Tap into images when you feel limited by your experiences. Allow your imagination to be invigorated by an essence when developing a character.

Avoid trying to be correct with the physicalization of images and essences. The most inspiring moments leading to a solid interpretation will happen when you are nonresistant. Flow with the image. The image will take you to new places. Exploring the essence of an object, nature, or music will focus your acting experience and liberate your imagination.

JOURNAL ENTRIES

Describe your experience using animal imagery with a characterization.

Describe your process and choices using images such as nature, season, events, objects, or colors, and your connections, for a character study.

Describe additional observations, impressions, and ideas for future reference.

What choices did you make using music with characterization? Describe the physical and psychological experiences.

CHARACTER: SPACE, TIME, WEIGHT, AND ACTION

SPACE AND CHARACTER

A character's spatial awareness and experience are basic factors that influence behavior. While a character is rarely conscious of using space as a means of nonverbal communication, you can make choices about space utilization that will help define a character for yourself and an audience.

PROJECT: CHARACTER AND SPATIAL RELATIONSHIPS

Select a scene and character. Analyze the scene for an objective, obstacle, actions, and given circumstances. Do not discuss your choices with your scene partner, but rather work from the moments of interplay. Use the case study of *True West* by Sam Shepard for this project or as a model.

1. Center as the character and feel a breath connection. As the breath flows in and out let it shape your alignment, placement, center, relaxation/tension, and attention to space.
2. Look about the space and physically respond to impressions. Are you in the middle of the space or more toward the periphery? Is there room overhead? Is the space open and airy or restrictive? Do you feel freedom to move or do you feel the need to be cautious? Physicalize.
3. Move through the space. Sense the use of direction, level, size, and shape.
4. Focus on using indirect and direct space. Attend the space. What draws your focus?
5. Pair up with an actor playing the other character. Move about each other sensing the spatial relationships. How does it feel to come in close proximity? To walk away? To be seated while the other is standing or lying down? Keep exploring all types of movement and spatial arrangements. Heighten your indirect

and direct spatial awareness. Move with your impulses.
6. Work with dialogue. Be specific about who you are and your objective, obstacle, and action. Focus on spatial relationships. Select qualitative and quantitative space factors to communicate your needs.

What did you find about the character's use of space when alone and when relating to the other with or without dialogue? How did the objectives and obstacles influence the use of space? What was your character's perception of the space? What changes were observed and discovered that could be channeled into the characterization and actions?

TIME AND CHARACTER

Time can be both intangible and measured. When working with the Laban time effort factors, you can make choices about a character's attitude toward time and circumstances. The quantitative factors of tempo, accents, rests, meter, and rhythm can be incorporated to create subtle yet powerful physical behaviors. The behaviors are not to be imposed, but rather need to evolve out of the acting process.

Explore the elements of time using a scripted character and scene. In doing so be reminded of the importance of carrying through a basic character analysis. Use the following exercises as illustrations of how the study of time might be used to help define a character, situation, or relationship.

PROJECT: CHARACTER AND TIME

Use the same scene and character as in the space project.

1. Review your objective, obstacle, and action. Is the character's attitude about time quick or sustained? Play, observe, explore, and discover the character's preferences.
2. Tempo: Focus on the tempo of the character's behavior. How fast or slow do you move? Why? What are you doing? Break down moment to moment a specific activity the character does. Play with various tempos as you continue to use the objective and action.
3. Rests: Some playwrights specifically define where pauses should occur. Playwrights write more than dialogue—they craft stories. A pause may indicate a shift in the dramatic action.

Work through a unit of action focusing on pauses or rests. Does the tempo build up to a pause? What happens during the pause? What does the use of the pause tell the audience about the character?

3. Accent: What movements can be stressed to emphasize the character's actions or relationship? In what way can the physical activity be accented to communicate the character's experience?
4. Meter: Use meter to find the pulse of the character. Select a piece of music that you feel has the underlying beat of the action. Play it and respond. Explore on your own before interacting with the other character. When both actors feel ready begin the unit of dialogue. Let yourself stay with the pulse of the music at first. Then abandon the conscious movement and let the character's movement evolve.

Discuss with your partner or observers insights that you gained about the unit of action, character, and relationship through the use of accents and meter. How does the element of time help in character definition?

WEIGHT AND CHARACTER

The study of weight and character may help you define the character's intentions. Laban defined weight's inner participation as being one of intention. The character's intention may be strong, forceful, heavy, or light, gentle, and tender. There are many degrees of weight that have both an inner attitude and physical expression.

Exercise: Weight and Character

1. Select a short scene or monologue and a character.
2. Make a choice about the character's preference for strong or light weight for the scene or monologue and then physicalize.
3. Create a movement score and heighten the weight effort influence.
4. Share the movement score with others for observation and discussion.

ACTION AND CHARACTER

Actions may fluctuate from scene to scene or moment to moment. While a chosen action may change as you develop the character and scene it is best to begin with one solid choice. Experiencing the action for a specific objective will provide a clear physical impulse.

Project: Action and Character

Refer to the case studies for an analysis of a scene between Antigone and Ismene from Anouilh's *Antigone* as a model.

1. Select a character and short scene for study. Center, focus, and incorporate alignment, breath, and state of being choices.
2. Select an action necessary for the scene's first beat. Indulge yourself in the action without using words. Begin moving one body area at a time. Add other areas, then the entire body. Add sound.
3. Work through the beat using the action as the primary movement force. Be bold and unconventional with behavior. Stay in the moment and respond to the other. Give and take.
4. Add phrases and then dialogue. Stop when needed to explore the dynamics and intensity for specific moments. Keep working until you are ready to let the beat flow without stopping.
5. Using the action's physical essence transform to conventional behavior appropriate for the world of the play.
6. Repeat this process for all the beats and build the scene.

What action changes does the character go through? How do dynamics or intensity adjust with each action? Play with the exploration and discovery process. Be specific with acting choices.

SUMMARY

The elements of space, time, weight, and action are primary movement factors. The movement potential and possibilities of these factors are numerous. After a script and character is complete be bold with the explorations. Be open to many choices. Work independently and at the same time in harmony with your scene partner. There are no rights and wrongs, but there are more vital and meaningful choices you can make through observation, exploration, discovery, and interpretation.

JOURNAL ENTRIES

Describe discoveries made about spatial relationships within a character or scene study.

Describe how the weight effort factor defined behavior for a specific acting assignment.

Describe an LMA action choice as part of the character's behavior.

Describe how the use of time defined your character's behavior or a moment of action.

Record additional observations, impressions, and ideas for future reference.

CHARACTER: ENVIRONMENT, PROPERTIES, AND COSTUMES

ENVIRONMENT

The audience experiences the environment through the actor/character. It is an actor's responsibility to make the environment real for the audience. Designers may provide visual and aural details for an audience and the actor needs to take advantage of every resource, but the ultimate responsibility is for the actor to bring the environment into existence.

Ask yourself questions about the environment. Seek details to have a clear understanding of where you are, and ask about your relationship to the environment. In the following projects you will work with a character while focusing on environment, properties, and costumes. Embody the character by focusing on alignment, breath, center.

Examine the importance of the environment in relation to characterization within a scene. After each portion of the process review your experience. Build the process by incorporating the use of the dialogue and action.

Refer to the case studies for environment, properties, and costumes projects for Sheridan's *The School for Scandal* as an approach and model for a character and scene of your choice.

Project: Environment and Character

Select a scene and character. Analyze the given circumstances with your scene partner. Review circumstances relating to the environment.

1. Build the environment through a detailed description with the other character. Move about the space as you describe where you are. Be specific. Create and respond to the sensory stimuli.
2. Be in the environment. Interact with the space, climate, and objects. Personalize the environment. What does the place mean to

you? Have you been here before? Do any of the objects have a significant history? What is the climate? Is it damp, cool, hot, dry, muggy, or do ideal conditions prevail? Physicalize.
3. Work through the character's activity and focus on using the environment to communicate the objective, obstacle, and action.
4. Create a movement study with your scene partner. Show where you are through movement.
5. Share your movement study with others.
6. Repeat the movement study and add dialogue.

How can the environment be used to help define a character? How does the environment impact the character's alignment, focus, breath, or center? In what ways does building a detailed environment help enrich the character's depth?

How do relationships change the concept of the environment? How did you use the environment to communicate with the other characters and the audience? Pinpoint what environmental elements are unclear and how they can be further defined.

PROPERTIES

The use of a property enlightens an audience about a character's inner life. A property can become an extension of the character by underscoring important actions and words. It can heighten the action and move the plot forward. Use properties with clarity and precision as dictated by the character's needs.

Project: Functional and Expressive Use of a Property

1. Select a character, monologue, and a hand property.

2. Explore the property with your senses.
3. Discover ways to use the property functionally and expressively. Interact with the environment. (Refer to the section in Part Two on the use of properties in a functional and expressive manner.)
4. Work with the monologue and use the property to underscore the action and the character's needs. Create functional and expressive uses within the scene. Be clear and precise when gesturing with a property. Decide where the activity begins. How does the movement end? What is the gesture's primary statement?
5. Work through the monologue focusing on the prop as an extension of the character. Share the monologue with others. Let them tell you what they saw about the property's use and characterization.

How can the property be an extension of the character? How did its usage provide visual clues about subtext or underscore the characterization?

To give the property's usage believability, personalize it. If it belongs to the character then know where it came from, how old it is, and if it has a personal significance. If it is a representation of a real object (such as an inexpensive tin ashtray representing a treasured gold ashtray), then handle it so the audience believes it has the qualities given in the script.

Project: Personalization of a Property

Use the same character and monologue as in the previous project. Select a moment in which a property is required but the actual property lacks one or more of the required characteristics. Example: The character is to sip scalding hot tea but instead you use room temperature water.

1. Work with the property as the character, and endow it with truthful movement qualities. Focus on the character's sensory and emotional perceptions. What is the object's texture? Describe its physical details. What does it smell like? Can it make sounds? When did you obtain it? Was it given to you? Did you personally select it? How long have you had it, or is this your first use of the object? Why are you handling it? What do you want? Does it have a functional use?

2. Integrate the prop's use with the monologue's objective, obstacle, and action. Build on the prop's functional and expressive usage.

After endowing the property with a history and personalization was its usage any different than before? How did the personalization affect the character's handling of it? What did you learn about the character and relationships? Record your impressions in the journal.

COSTUMES

Because the costume is personal and part of the character's identity the actor must give it meaning and significance. Know its history. Did you select the fabrics and have the garment made for you? Was it chosen for a special occasion, as an everyday work uniform, or as an afterthought? Have you worn it before? How often? Does the clothing have any special meaning? Keep asking yourself questions to realize a firm understanding of why your character is wearing these particular clothing articles. Consider period, customs, social values, work ethics, and the economic, political, and religious circumstances.

With any costume first take time to examine the garment. Look at how it is constructed. Where are the seams? How do they affect joint dexterity? In what parts of the body will movement be restricted? Is it heavy, light, rough, smooth, form-fitting, nonclinging, rigid, or flowing? Does it move with you, or do you have to carry it about? Does it make you feel comfortable, stuffy, a spectacle, or restricted in any way? Again, keep asking yourself questions to better understand how to move in the costume to make it truthful, believable, and part of the character's identity.

In most plays the costume is more than decoration or ornamentation. It is the actor's responsibility to make the costume speak for the character. A costume is part of a character's identity. The acting process is enlivened when the costume is regarded as an asset. Don't fight against the costume, but rather use it to help understand the character. Determine how the garment can work for you. Look at what it says about the character, play, environment, and concept of the production. How can it help you in portraying the character?

Using a rehearsal costume is strongly recommended if the costume is of a different period or style than you are used to wearing. For instance, if you are not accustomed to wearing a long skirt, corset, high heels, armor, short pants, etc., it is difficult to adjust during the first dress rehearsal and be ready to perform on opening night. Secure a rehearsal costume well in advance before the first dress rehearsal. Spend time in front of a full-length mirror and look at your image, silhouette, and how you move in the costume. By using a rehearsal costume you can overcome unforeseen blocking challenges and obstacles if the costume is not worn before the week of performance.

Project: Costume and Character

Part One: Shoes

1. Select a character, monologue, and a pair of shoes. Use your senses to explore the shoes. Know their movement limitations and possibilities. Stand, walk, run, skip, etc. How do the shoes adjust your alignment, placement, height, sense of weight, walking patterns, and image.
2. Remove the shoes. Center as the character.
3. Pick up the shoes and look at them. Talk about what they mean to you. Are they for practicality or adventure? Did you buy them or have them made? What do you like or dislike about the shoes?
4. Put the shoes on and move. Let the shoes adjust your alignment, placement, weight, focus, and energy. Perform the character's activities.
5. Work through the monologue and let the shoes influence behavior and mannerisms.

How did the shoes influence the character's behavior? How did they impact the physical mannerisms?

Part Two: Garment

Choose a garment the character would wear. If the playwright does not describe the dress create the character's apparel based on given circumstances.

1. Look at the garment closely. How is it constructed? Why is it appropriate for the character?
2. Put the garment on and study your image in a mirror. Who are you? What do you want the world to experience? What do you think they see? Why?
3. Personalize the garment. Know its history and meaning.
4. Move about finding the garment's potential and limitations. Does the garment flow with you? Do you feel its texture and weight? Does it provide any conflict by limiting movement the character would like to do?
5. Come to an alignment, placement, and centering based on the character's objectives, qualities, and costume.
6. Incorporate the environment. Move as the character in the environment and with a given situation.
7. How does the costume help reinforce the stance, manner of sitting, walking, and gesturing?
8. Use the garment to communicate the character's needs by, say, using it with a gesture to emphasize an emotion or viewpoint. It may be the way you twirl the hem of a skirt, button a shirt, or adjust a jacket or sleeve. It is working with the garment's overall image and impact in addition to the gestural details that give the character depth.

When working with a different time period first approach the character's identity and needs. No matter what period the play takes place in human nature is much the same. The manners and movement will be dictated by the time's social and moral customs. Look at the furniture the characters have to move around or use, the music they listen to, the literature they read, and the architecture that surrounds them. Find out whatever you can about the period to better understand why they moved as they did. Incorporate your findings into the activity, but do not superimpose or impede behavior unless it is grounded in the character's life. Your task is to be true to the play and the character while incorporating period manners to inform behavior.

SUMMARY

The use of environment, properties, and costumes can provide invaluable insight for the actor and audience about the character. These tools can say through movement much more than words can. Invest in the use of these tools. Take time to explore each element to be objective about their functions within the entire production. Know the movement possibilities around and within the environment, the functional and expressive use of a property, and that a costume is more than body decoration.

Describe how you used a costume to define a character's behavior.

JOURNAL ENTRIES

What did you discover about characterization and environment?

Describe a way that you used a property to define a character and a moment of action.

Process additional observations, impressions, and ideas for future reference.

CASE STUDIES

The following are sample case studies to be used as references for various projects in Part Three. To better comprehend each case study it is advisable to read the cited play. If you choose other characters for projects these studies can illustrate how to link movement concepts and choices to characterizations.

RELAXATION AND CHARACTER

The Glass Menagerie: A Case Study
Project: Character Study Using the Seven States of Being

Even when a character is not engaged in heavy or strenuous physical activity varying degrees of relaxation and tension are present. Some of the more sensational moments in drama are those in which there is very little physical activity but the action is intense. For example, in Tennessee Williams's play *The Glass Menagerie,* when Jim enters the room where Laura has been resting during dinner the atmosphere is filled with tension. This meeting marks the climax in Laura's secret life. Laura's physical activity is sitting on the sofa, but her state of being is highly charged with fear and desire, which results in high tension levels.

Consider her objectives, obstacles, actions, and her emotional and physical attributes for the entire play, then scene by scene.

Refer to scenes 6 and 7 to examine Laura's levels of relaxation and tension moment to moment. Note how Laura goes through a complex array of changes. At the beginning of scene 6, Laura and Amanda are preparing for the gentleman caller. Laura is nervous because of the fuss that Amanda is going through. Laura feels that they are plotting to deceive the visitor, and she wants to escape Amanda's plan. Laura is more tense than normal,

but she is stable. Her composure begins to unravel when Amanda tells her that the gentleman caller's name is Jim O'Connor. Laura fears that it is the same Jim O'Connor she had a crush on in high school. As she thinks about this possibility her tension level begins to rise. Amanda tells Laura that she must open the door when her brother and Jim arrive. This causes Laura to panic.

Her tension intensifies when the doorbell rings. When she opens the door and meets Jim she is terrified. She can barely speak and remain composed at the same time, so she leaves the room. By the time dinner is served Laura's anxiety is so intense that she becomes ill and must retire to the living room to lie down while the others eat. In each beat the tension level increases until Laura must lie down.

Scene 7 takes place after dinner. The electricity has been disconnected. Jim enters the living room with a candelabrum. Laura feels somewhat protected hiding in the partial darkness, and her tension decreases. She grows more confident and in control as she asks Jim about his singing and talks about the past. Laura's memories of the past have provided an escape from reality over the last several years. As she and Jim go farther into the memory of years past Laura's tensions continue to decrease. Her tension changes when she learns that Jim did not marry his high school sweetheart Emily Meisenbach.

Jim asks Laura about what she has done since high school. This introduces a reality that Laura would like to avoid. She changes the subject to her glass collection, an area of escape and comfort. Laura's tension intensifies when Jim asks her to dance. She has never danced with anyone, much less think that she might someday be this close to Jim. Williams called it the "climax of her life." Her world of illusion and reality are beginning to blend together.

Laura's most prized piece of glass is broken

during the dance. To Laura it is only momentarily traumatic. The reason she is not more tense is because of her euphoria about being with Jim. Jim kisses Laura and she sinks onto the couch. For a short time she doesn't seem to hear or see anything. At this moment everything is harmonious and she is at peace.

This shows how a character's tension levels change from moment to moment. The tension and intensity may vary depending on the circumstances. When Laura's glass ornament is dropped her tension is of a different nature than when Jim enters the room with the candelabrum.

Use this case study as a model when analyzing how varying degrees of relaxation and tension may have a physical impact upon a character. If you are in a class, discuss a character from a play the class has seen or read and focus on the concept of relaxation and characterization. Discuss how using the Seven States of Being can be incorporated in a rehearsal process.

ALIGNMENT AND CHARACTER

As You Like It: A Case Study
Project: Alignment Changes Within a Monologue

Analyzing Rosalind in Shakespeare's *As You Like It* as a study in alignment presents an interesting challenge because of her disguise and pretense of being a man in acts 2, 3, and 4. Being the daughter of Duke Senior, the former ruler, she is a lady of the court. She is well educated and leads a life of relative leisure. However, in act 1 she is troubled. When Rosalind is first seen she is with her cousin Celia, who asks Rosalind to be merry. Rosalind replies: "Dear Celia, I show more mirth than I am mistress of, and would you yet I were merrier? "

Throughout act 1, scene 3 Rosalind is disturbed about her father's absence and her future in Arden. A major development in Rosalind's life is meeting Orlando. She falls in love at first sight. What alignment changes might occur after her spirits are lifted by the hope of uniting with Orlando? Rosalind's next crisis is when Duke Frederick, her uncle, banishes her from court. She decides to disguise herself as a man and run away to the forest. Celia joins her in the plan and both tell of their forthcoming deceit. Rosalind declares:

> Were it not better,   110
> Because that I am more than common tall,
> That I did suit me all points like a man?
> A gallant curtle-axe upon my thigh,
> A boar-spear in my hand; and, in my heart
> Lie there what hidden woman's fear there will,
> We'll have a swashing and martial outside,
> As many other mannish cowards have
> That do outface it with their semblances.

This dialogue may provide a starting point for Rosalind's alignment when disguised and pretending to be a man.

In the forest Rosalind has taken the name of Ganymede. She soon learns that Orlando has also sought refuge in the country and has been hanging love verses on the trees and carving Rosalind's name into the barks. Rosalind wants to be sure Orlando is truly in love with her, so she decides that she will remain in her male attire and approach him. She tells Celia: "I will speak to him like a saucy lackey, and under the habit play the knave with him." She enjoys the pretense and decides to go much farther with it when she tells Orlando that she (Ganymede) will pretend to be a woman and he will come to court her each day. In doing so she will cure him of his lovesick passion. In act 3, scene 2 Orlando questions whether she has ever cured anyone before, she answers:

> Yes, one and in this manner. He was to imagine me his love, his mistress; and I set him every day to woo me. At which time would I, being but a moonish youth grieve, be effeminate, changeable, longing and liking, proud, fantastical, apish, shallow, inconstant, full of tears, full of smiles; for every passion something and for no passion truly anything, as boys and women are for the most part cattle of this color; would now like him, now loathe him; then entertain him, then forswear him; now weep for him, then spit at him; that I drove my suitor from his mad humor of love to a living humor of madness, which was, to forswear the full stream of the world and to live in a nook merely monastic. And thus I cured him; and this way will I take upon me to wash your liver clean as a sound sheep's heart, that there shall not be one spot of love in't.

Not a glowing description of female behavior, but Rosalind is attempting to win Orlando's trust and interest. What can be noted and used is the contrast of her description of female disposition with that of the male's, which she described earlier. The dialogue can provide the key to perception and behavior in relation to alignment choices.

Reviewing the circumstances within the story and the impact on Rosalind's alignment you will see what an important element environment plays. In court she is a victim, made to suffer because of her heritage. In the country she is a subjugator as she pursues Orlando. In court she feels trapped, and in the country she is free. By virtue of necessity she must be bold to meet the adversity in Duke Frederick's court, but in the country she has many opportunities to experience delight and let down her guard. She feels that she can take more risks as Ganymede because of her masculine disguise. Her perceptions of male behavior equate to more liberties. She has two distinct views of the world based on her environment, and these have an impact on her alignment.

BREATH AND CHARACTER

Arms and the Man: A Case Study
Project: Character and Breath

Analyze the first scene between Raina and Bluntschli in George Bernard Shaw's *Arms and the Man* to explore how breath is connected to characterization.

It is a November night in 1885 in Bulgaria. The action takes place in Raina's bedchamber, which Shaw describes as "half rich and half cheap Viennese." The room contains a bed, dresser, and ottoman, and has a large window that leads out to a balcony. When the action begins Raina is looking out the window and dreaming of her love Sergius, who is a soldier in the Bulgarian army fighting Serbian forces. The sounds of war are in the distance, but Raina doesn't seem to notice or comprehend the danger. She goes to bed after kissing a picture of Sergius and vows "I shall never be unworthy of you any more, my soul's hero: never, never, never." She leaves one candle lit as she crawls into bed to read a romance novel. A distant shot is heard. She hears more fusillades as the sound of war comes closer to her home. She quickly jumps out of bed to blow out the candle and retreats to safety under her blankets and pillows. Next she hears the shutters opening and can see a man's silhouette on the balcony.

The man is Bluntschli, a Serbian soldier. He is running away from the battle and searching for refuge. Raina calls out "Who's there? Who's there? Who is

that?" Bluntschli threatens "Sh!—Sh! Don't call out; or you'll be shot. Be good; and no harm will happen to you."

How is breath linked with communication in the moment Bluntschli and Raina first meet? What impact does the immediacy of danger have on each of them? If breath affects movement, and vice versa, how might it be manifested? The exercise may be used as an outline for any character of your choice.

The Glass Menagerie: A Case Study

In scene 3 Amanda and Tom have an argument that most likely has been repeated numerous times. Amanda has a "choke hold" on Tom's existence, and he is struggling to remain alive. Tom finally lashes out at his mother with lies, which she believes but doesn't want to hear. Refer to Amanda's dialogue: "What right have you got to jeopardize your job? Jeopardize the security of us all? How do you think we'd manage if you were. . . ." And her final line of the scene: "I won't speak to you—until you apologize!"

Imagine that you are rehearsing the scene and having difficulty releasing your emotions, phrasing your breath with dialogue and action, or unable to maintain your characterization. Based on your observations, explorations, discoveries, and knowledge realized from the exercises in parts One and Two, how could breath help you make the missing connection?

If you were playing Amanda ask yourself "What am I feeling that makes me want to accuse Tom of being a liar, and not living up to his responsibilities?" As Tom ask "What am I feeling as I lie to my mother?" As each character answer the following questions and physicalize the answers using breath as the impulse. What is my objective? What is my obstacle? What am I willing to do to get what I want?

CENTER AND CHARACTER

Summer and Smoke: A Case Study
Project: Character Center and Choice

In part 1, scene 2, of Williams's *Summer and Smoke*, Alma is struggling for survival, trying to cope with a world in which she feel she doesn't belong. In a desperate attempt to survive she sees the doctor next door,

Dr. John Buchanan, Sr. She tells him that she doesn't think she'll survive the summer, but that if she does she will be terribly changed somehow. She has been offered a marriage proposal from Roger Doremus, and she subconsciously wants to be advised against accepting. She doesn't realize that her symptoms are psychological and seeks medical (or physical) attention to relieve her anxieties.

Alma is behaving with a predominant survival center. Her basic need is for survival. Although she is in no immediate danger she has a growing concern about what she is going to do with the rest of her life. She is beginning to feel old. Her immediate sense of survival is to get through the rest of the summer. She feels that if she can get that far something will happen to change her circumstances. Near the end of the scene she says, "We've all of us got to be patient. At least till the end of summer. If we can go that far, we can go much further, and somewhere, sometime—there must be some revelation, the visit of some angel to straighten things out." Alma is searching for enlightenment.

The play takes place over the entire summer. In part 1, scene 5, Alma returns to the doctor's office, this time in hopes of seeing Dr. John Buchanan, Jr. In this scene Alma exhibits conflicting needs. She desires John sexually but can't come to terms with it on a psychological level. Instead, she allows her intellect to suppress her physical desire and decorates it instead in the guise of spiritual love, thus basing her actions on the heart center.

In part 2, scene 5, Alma finally comes to terms with the reality of who she is and what she wants. She returns to John, even though she knows he is engaged to someone else, to confront him with the truth. She is enlightened of her own sexual awareness and desire and has finally opened the channels that allow her to see and think clearly. Alma is in her greatest state of balance at this point. She has had the revelation she described in scene 2 and will now continue her life with a conscious awareness of her needs. She is grounded in her power center, the solar plexus.

IMAGERY AND CHARACTER

The Glass Menagerie: A Case Study
Project: Event, Object, Color, and Character

In scene 2 of *The Glass Menagerie* Laura tells Amanda that she has been wandering about for weeks instead of attending secretarial school, and feels ashamed. Visualize a color that represents Laura's or Amanda's essence. Color imagery is often used to describe attitude (feeling blue, green with envy, seeing red). Create an essence study based on the character and color selected.

Another example of connecting imagery and essence studies to characterization is to use an object's essence as the movement impulse. Look at the moment just before Amanda enters scene 2 when she confronts Laura. When Laura hears Amanda approaching she sets aside her glass figures and sits in front of the typewriter and a secretarial diagram pretending to study. Amanda enters and removes her gloves. From her purse she removes a handkerchief, shakes it out, and touches it to her lips and nostrils. Crossing slowly to the wall, she removes the diagram and holds it in front of her for a second. She stares at it and then maliciously rips it in half.

This detailed description is taken from Williams's narrative. He saw Amanda's physical response to the diagram as central to effective communication. The actor can enrich the moment by playing with the images the object creates. What does the diagram represent to Laura and Amanda? How might Laura physically react to Amanda's action? Select either character or another of your choice and create a movement study focusing on what the diagram represents.

SPACE, TIME, WEIGHT, ACTION, AND CHARACTER

True West: A Case Study
Project: Character and Spatial Relationships

The action of Sam Shepard's *True West* takes place in the kitchen of an older home in a southern California suburb. It is a realistic setting with a sink, refrigerator, counter, cupboards, table and chairs, window, and phone.

The home's owner is in Alaska, and her son Austin is using the house for business. His brother Lee is visiting. Austin has come to California to write and negotiate the sale of a script to a movie producer. He is near to completing the deal, and feels pressure to write. Lee has been living in the desert, needs money, and has come to town to burglarize area homes.

At the beginning of the action Austin is mildly irritated by Lee's presence. He needs to be writing but Austin continues to interrupt his work. Austin is preparing to meet with Saul, a producer, and has asked Lee to leave the house during the meeting. Lee returns early and has a chance to talk to Saul about a story he has in mind for a movie project. In act 2, scene 5, Lee tells Austin that Saul has decided to produce his story instead of Austin's. Review the scene as an example of how spatial awareness and usage can help define character choices.

Review act 2, scene 9, of *True West.* The home has been trashed by Austin and Lee. The brothers have been working on Lee's movie script and are irritated with each other. The mother returns home as Lee is pouring beer on his body to cool off, and Austin is absorbed in his writing. Work through this scene and discover movement choices based on qualitative and quantitative space elements.

Antigone: A Case Study
Project: Actions and Character

Study the scene between Antigone and Ismene in Anouilh's *Antigone* when Antigone has just returned from burying the corpse of her brother Polynices. She has decided to defy Creon's decree forbidding a religious burial. Ismene, unaware of Antigone's fatal actions, is determined to make Antigone realize how dangerous it would be to act against Creon. Ismene paints a picture of haunting terror, torture, and death.

Ismene: His mob will come running, howling as it runs. A thousand arms will seize our arms. A thousand breaths will breathe into our faces. Like one single pair of eyes, a thousand eyes will stare at us. We'll be driven in a tumbrel through their hatred, through the smell of them and their cruel, roaring laughter. We'll be dragged to the scaffold for torture, surrounded by guards, with their idiot faces all bloated, their animal hands clean-washed for the sacrifice, their beefy eyes squinting as they stare at us. And we'll know that no shrieking and no begging will make them understand that we want to live, for they are like slaves who do exactly as they've been told, without caring about right or wrong. And we shall suffer, we shall feel pain rising in us until it becomes so unbearable that we know it must stop. But it won't stop it will go on rising and rising, like a screaming voice, Oh, I can't, I can't, Antigone!

Ismene needs to save her sister's life. Her conflict is Antigone's strength and will, her own self-doubt, and physical weariness from lack of sleep. Her desires lead her to use fear, shame, and severing family ties as tactics.

If you were to play Ismene at the moment Antigone has just returned after burying Polynices, what action choices would you explore to discover behaviors? Look at the entire scene and ask questions about how Antigone's actions are different from Ismene's. How does one character respond to the other?

Experience the character's dynamics, intensity, and action changes. At the beginning Antigone is physically and mentally drained from sneaking out to bury her brother. Ismene is on edge as a result of being awake all night trying to decide the right course of action. As the sisters talk Ismene becomes more intense in her need to save Antigone from making a horrible mistake. She tries several actions in pursuit of her objective, and with each new action a new dynamic force comes into play.

Throughout the scene Antigone is defiant. She progresses through several dynamic changes that alter her rebellious attitude. At first she seems reserved and distant. After Ismene asks "Don't you want to go on living?" Antigone explodes with anger. She addresses Ismene with shame. Ismene is shaken and attempts to reveal to Antigone how beautiful life will be with Haemon. Antigone is resolved to do what is honorable. By the end of the scene both sisters have retreated. Use this scene as a reference or model to define action choices and behavior.

ENVIRONMENT, PROPERTIES, COSTUMES, AND CHARACTER

The School for Scandal: A Case Study
Project: Environment and Character

As an example of linking environment to scripted characters, look at one of the most famous scenes in English drama, the "screen scene" in *The School for Scandal* by Richard Brinsley Sheridan. In this scene Lady Teazle has come to seek the confidence of Joseph Surface, a scandalmonger.

They are in his library when her husband, Sir Peter Teazle, arrives. Lady Teazle hides behind a screen just before Sir Peter's entrance. Sir Peter discusses Lady

Teazle's honesty and loyalty with Joseph. Awareness about the environment is heightened for Joseph knowing that Lady Teazle is listening to every word. It becomes increasingly uncomfortable when Sir Peter brings up Joseph's interest in Maria, Sir Peter's ward. The tension builds when Charles Surface, Joseph's brother, enters. At this point Sir Peter decides to withdraw behind the screen, but Joseph says a French milliner is hiding there and it would be best to hide in the closet. The scene continues with the husband and wife in separate hiding places. Later in the scene Joseph reveals Sir Peter. After Joseph leaves Charles and Sir Peter decide to unveil the French milliner. The appearance of Lady Teazle in Joseph Surface's home demands a great deal of explanation to satisfy Sir Peter's curiosity.

The School for Scandal: A Case Study
Project: Functional and Expressive Use of Properties

Review act 5, scene 2, of *The School for Scandal* for a study of character and properties. In this scene, the "screen scene," Mrs. Candor, Sir Benjamin Backbite, Lady Sneerwell, and Crabtree have gathered to gossip about the events that occurred in Sir Joseph's library. Each one elaborates more fully than the other about the scandal until they declare that a duel took place and Charles Surface and the Postman were both struck by bullets. Use the exercises to discover functional and expressive property usage and personaliza-tion with characters from this scene. You might use a cane, handkerchief, snuff box, fan, cakes, cookies, and/or a tea service. How can the property's use aid in character definition? Share the scene and characters and discuss.

The School for Scandal
Project: Costume and Character

Act 3, scene 1, of *The School for Scandal* provides a rich study for scripted characters and costumes. In this scene Sir Peter and Lady Teazle banter about money, marriage, betrayal, and divorce. The scene begins with the couple in harmonious agreement but ends with threats of separation. A major turning point in the scene is when Lady Teazle asks for money. Sir Peter accuses her of being ill-tempered, and then suggests that she and Charles Surface have been having an affair. Sir Peter's suspicions about the romance prompt him to seek the advice of Joseph Surface, which leads to the "screen scene" discussed earlier.

How can the costumes be used to illustrate the change of each character's demeanor? How does the character carry the garment's weight and style? How does movement and use of the garment and/or shoes help define the character? What special significance do the garments have for a character?

Select a character and create a nonverbal movement study utilizing the costume to define character behavior.

CONCLUSION

Each individual's behaviors are shaped by physical, intellectual, and psychological characteristics, which are integrated in the interest of expressing an autonomous self. This text has focused on movement concepts, or drawing upon the self as a means of expression for enhancing a character. Bridging the person to actor to character has been addressed in the form of practical exercises and projects to be used as fundamental tools for continued growth.

Perhaps the most important conclusion to draw is that the discovery process is perpetual; it cannot progress from beginning to end in a series of logical, precise steps. Humanity dictates that we are in a constant state of change, and each change alters perception and the field of choices. These moments between the beginning and ending mark discoveries that can lead to an actor's perpetual growth. Acting and movement should not be considered mediums in which a true pinnacle exists. Instead, they are a process within which growth has no boundaries. As George Plimpton said, "Do not strive for the pursuit of happiness: that way lies grief. Concentrate instead upon the happiness of the pursuit."

It is my hope that this text has served as a foundation for more in-depth movement studies, and ultimately a basis from which personal ideas and conclusions can be drawn.

BIBLIOGRAPHY

Alter, Judy. *Stretch & Strengthen.* Boston: Houghton Mifflin Company, 1986.

Alter, Michael J. *Science of Stretching.* Champaign, IL: Human Kinestics Books, 1988.

American Heritage Dictionary of the English Language, New College Edition. New York: American Heritage Publishing Co., Inc., and Houghton Mifflin Company, 1975.

Anodea, Judith. *Wheels of Life.* St. Paul, MN: Llewellyn Publications, 1990.

Barker, Sarah. *The Alexander Technique.* New York: Bantam Books, Inc., 1978.

Barlow, Wilfred. *The Alexander Technique.* New York: Warner Books Inc., 1973.

Bartenieff, Irmgard. with Dori Lewis. *Body Movement: Coping with the Environment.* Gordon and Breach Science Publishers, 1993.

Benedetti, Robert. *The Actor at Work.* Englewood Cliffs, NJ: Prentice-Hall, 1976.

Beryl, Frank. *Dictionary of Nutrition and Food Values.* New York: Galahad Books, 1981.

Brody, Jane. *New York Times Guide to Personal Health.* New York: Times Books, 1982.

Chaikin, Joseph. *The Presence of the Actor.* New York: Atheneum, 1972.

Chekhov, Michael. *To the Actor: On the Technique of Acting.* New York: Harper and Row Publishers, Inc., 1953.

Cohen, Robert. *Acting One.* Palo Alto, CA: Mayfield Publishing Company, 1984.

Crawford, Jerry L. *Acting in Person and in Style,* Second Edition. Dubuque, IA: Wm. C. Brown Company, 1976.

Dennis, Anne. *The Articulate Body.* New York: Drama Book Publishers, 1995.

Dominguez, Richard H. *The Complete Book of Sports Medicine.* New York: Warner Books, Inc., 1979.

Feldenkrais, Moshe. *Awareness Through Movement.* New York: Harper & Row, 1977.

Felner, Mira. *Free to Act.* New York: Holt, Rinehart and Winston, 1990.

Hagan, Uta. *Respect for Acting.* New York: Macmillan Publishing Co., Inc., 1973.

Jones, Frank Pierce. *Body Awareness in Action.* New York: Schocken Books, 1979.

King, Nancy. *A Movement Approach to Acting.* Englewood Cliffs, NJ: Prentice-Hall Inc., 1981.

_____. *Theatre Movement: The Actor and His Space.* New York: Drama Book Specialists, 1971.

Klein, Maxine. *Time, Space, and Designs for Actors.* Boston, MA: Houghton Mifflin Co., 1975.

Laban, Rudolf. *The Mastery of Movement.* London: MacDonald and Evans Limited, 1971.

Lessac, Arthur. *Body Wisdom: The Use and Training of the Human Body.* New York: Drama Book Publishers, 1981.

Linklater, Kristin. *Freeing the Natural Voice.* New York: Drama Book Specialists, 1976.

Minton, Sandra. *Modern Dance: Body and Mind.* Englewood, CO: Morton Publishing Company, 1984.

Passoli, Robert. *A Book on the Open Theatre.* Indianapolis: Bobbs-Merrill, 1976.

Penrod, James. *Movement for the Performing Artist.* Palo Alto, CA: Mayfield Publishing Co., 1974.

Phaneuf, Cindy Melby. "An Ensemble Process of Actor Training," *Theatre Southwest Journal* (May 1985): 13–19.

Pisk, Litz. *The Actor and His Body.* London: Harrap & Co. Ltd., 1975.

Newlove, Jean. *Laban for Actors and Dancers.* New York: Routledge, 1993.

Rockwood, Jerome. *The Craftsmen of Dionysus: An Approach to Acting.* Glenview, IL: Scott, Foresman and Co., 1966.

Rood, Arnold. *Gordon Craig on Movement and Dance.* Brooklyn, NY: Dance Horizons, 1977.

Rose, Mark V. *The Actor and His Double.* Chicago: Actor Training and Research Institute Press, 1986.

Rubin, Lucille S., ed. *Movement for the Actor.* New York: Drama Book Specialists, 1980.

Sabatine, Jean. *Movement Training for the Stage and Screen.* New York: Back Stage Books, 1995.

_____. *The Actor's Image.* Englewood Cliffs, NJ: Prentice-Hall, Inc., 1963.

Shawn, Ted. *Every Little Movement.* Brooklyn, NY: Dance Horizons, Inc., 1963.

Sherbon, Elizabeth. *On the Count of One.* Palo Alto, CA: Mayfield Publishing Company, 1982.

Spolin, Viola. *Improvisation for the Theatre.* Evanston, IL: Northwestern University Press, 1973.

Stanislavski, Constantin. *Building a Character*. New York: Theatre Arts Books, 1949.

Stewart, Gordon W. *Every Body's Fitness Book*. Ganges, British Columbia, Canada: 3 S Publishers, 1982.

Sullivan, Claudia N. *The Actor Moves*. Jefferson, NC: McFarland and Co., Inc., 1990.

Vickery, Donald M., and James F. Fries. *Take Care of Yourself*. Reading, MA: Addison-Wesley Publishing Co., 1977.

PLAYS CITED

Anouilh, Jean. *Antigone*. (1944)
Shakespeare, William. *As You Like It*. (1599)
Shaw, George Bernard. *Arms and the Man*. (1898)
Sheridan, Richard Brinsley. *The School for Scandal*. (1777)

Shepard, Sam. *True West*. (1981)
Williams, Tennessee. *The Glass Menagerie*. (1945)
———. *Summer and Smoke*. (1948)

INDEX

accent, 68
action, 69–71, 79, 96, 107
    case study application, 107
action drives, 69–70
The Actor Moves (Claudia N. Sullivan), 34
Alexander, F.M., 39
alignment, 32, 83
    actor, 34–35
    case study application, 104–105
    character use of, 83–84, 104–105
    exercises, 32–37, 83–84
    person, 32–33
animal behavior, 58, 91
Anouilh, Jean, 96, 197
Antigone (Anouilh, Jean), 96, 107
    case study application, 107
arm, 11–12
    exercises, 12
Arms and the Man (George Bernard Shaw), 85
    case study, 105
As You Like It (William Shakespeare), 83, 104
    case study application, 104–105
athletic training, 20

basic effort actions, 69–71
breath, 39, 48, 51
    actor, 50
    case study application, 105
    character use of, 85–86, 105
        exercises, 39–45, 48, 51, 85–86
    person, 39
    phrasing breath with movement, 42–45
body, 5, 19
    care, 19
Brody, Jane, 22
Building of a Character (Constanstin Stanislavski), 34

center, 47, 87
    actor, 48–50
    case study application, 105–106
    character use of, 87–88, 105–106
    exercises, 47–50, 87–88
    person, 47
Chaiken, Joseph, 53

character, 79
Chekhov, Michael, 48, 88
clavical, 9, 11
climate, 74
collarbone, 9
color, 52, 55, 92–93
cooling down, 19, 20
costume, 76–77, 100–101
    case study application, 108
    character use of, 100–101, 108
    garments, 77, 101
    personal preferences, 76
    shoes, 76–77, 101
Crow, Aileen, 34

dab action drive, 70
diet, 22
direction,
dynamics, 71

Effort, 63, 67, 68, 69
emotion, 1, 5, 39, 48
endurance, 20, 21
energy, 20, 27
environment, 73–74, 99
    actor, 75
    case study application, 107–108
    character use of, 99, 105, 107–108
    climate, 74
    exercises, 73–74, 99
    person, 73–74
essence, 56

Feldenkrais, Moshe, 34
femur, 12, 13
flexibility, 20, 21, 22
flick action drive, 70
float action drive, 70
foot, 13, 14
    exercise, 14
Freeing the Natural Voice (Kristin Linklater), 30, 39

garments, 77
given circumstances, 79

Glass Menagerie, The (Tennessee Williams), 1, 81, 85, 92, 103–104
   case study applications, 103–104, 105, 106
glide action drive, 70

head, 5, 6, 7

imagery, 41, 48, 55, 91–93
   animal behavior use of, 58, 91
   case study application, 106
   character use of, 91–93, 106
   color, 55, 92–93
   elements of nature, 57–58, 91, 92
   essence, 56–57, 60, 61
   events, 60–61, 92
   exercises, 55–61, 91–93
   music, 59–60, 93
   nonmusical sounds, 60, 93
   object, 57, 92
   seasons, 56, 92
injury prevention, 19, 20, 22–23
intensity, 71

knee, 13, 14
   exercise, 14

Laban, Rudolf, 63, 96
Laban movement analysis (LMA), 63, 70
Lecoq, Jacques, 30
leg, 13, 14
   exercise, 14
levels, 64–65
ligament, 17
Linklater, Kristin, 30, 39
Luthe M.D., Wolfgang, 28

meter, 68
Movement for the Actor (Lucille S. Rubin ed.), 34
Movement Training for the Stage and Screen (Jean Sabatine), 56
muscle(s), 15–17, 27
   coordination, 17
   fatigue, 21
   soreness, 17
   strength, 17, 26
music, 59–60

neutral, 34
New York Times Guide to Personal Health (Jane Brody), 22
nutrition, 22

objective, 79
obstacle, 79

pelvis, 10, 12, 13
   exercise, 12
placement, 35, 76
Plimpton, George, 109
press action drive, 70
properties, 74–75, 99–100
   actor use of, 74–76
   case study application, 108
   character use of, 99–100, 108
   expressive use of, 75, 108
   functional use of, 75, 108
punch action drive, 70

range of motion,
relaxation, 27
   actor use of, 29
   autogenic exercise, 28
   case study application, 103–104
   character use of, 80–81
   exercises, 27–30
   personal use of, 27–29
   progressive, 28
   seven states of being, 30, 103, 104
      character exercise, 81
rests, 68
rhythm, 68
rib cage, 9
   exercise, 9

Sabatine, Jean, 56
salute to the sun, 42–45
School for Scandal, The (Richard Brinsley Sheridan), 99, 107, 108
   case study applications, 107, 108
Schultz, M.D., Johannes, 28
seasons, 56
Seven States of Being, 30
   character exercise, 81
shape, 9, 83, 84
Shepard, Sam, 95, 106
Sheridan, Richard Brinsley, 107, 108
shoes, 76–77
shoulder, 9, 11, 12
   exercise, 12
skeleton, 5, 14, 32
skull, 6
slash action drive, 70
sound and movement, 45, 50, 51–54, 89–90
   actor use of, 52–53
   character use of, 89–90
   exercises, 51–54, 89–90
   from center, 52
   person, 52–53
space, 63–67
   case study application, 106–107

character use of, 95, 106–107
   direct effort, 63
   direction, 64
   exercises, 63–67, 95
   indirect effort, 63, 64
   levels, 64
   qualitative space, 63
   quantitative space, 64
   range of motion, 65
spatial relationships, 66–67, 95
spine, 7
   exercise, 8–9
Stanislavski, Constantin, 34
strength, 17, 20, 21
   training, 17, 21
stretch, 21, 22
   active, 22
   passive, 22
Sullivan, Claudia N., 34
Summer and Smoke (Tennessee Williams), 87,
   105–106
   case study application, 105–106

tan tien, 48
tempo,
tendon, 17
tension, 8, 9, 27, 30
   relaxation and, 27, 28
thigh, 12, 13

exercises, 12
time, 67–68, 95–96
   accent, 68, 96
   character use of, 95–96
   meter, 68, 96
   qualitative, 67
   quantitative, 67–68
   quick time effort, 67
   rests, 68, 96
   rhythm, 68
   sustained time effort, 67
   tempo, 68
To The Actor (Michael Chekhov), 48, 88
torso, 10
True West (Sam Shepard), 95, 106, 107

walk, 34
warming up, 19, 20
weight, 68–69, 96
   character use of, 96
   exercises, 69, 96
   heavy weight, 69
   light weight, 69
   light weight effort, 69
   qualitative weight, 68
   quantitative weight, 69
   strong weight effort, 68–69
Williams, Tennessee, 1, 85, 103, 106
wring action drive, 70

ABOUT THE AUTHOR

Theresa Mitchell is an associate professor at the Conservatory of Theatre Arts at Webster University where she is the head of the performance program and director of the Webster Movement Institute. She is the past president of the Association of Theatre Movement Educators.